CHRISTIAN SYMBOLISM
In the Evangelical Churches

Doorway of Chapel, First Methodist
Church, Evanston, Illinois

CHRISTIAN SYMBOLISM
in the
Evangelical Churches

WITH DEFINITIONS OF
CHURCH TERMS AND USAGES

By

THOMAS ALBERT STAFFORD

With an Introduction by
ERNEST FREMONT TITTLE

Illustrated by the Author

ABINGDON PRESS
New York ● *Nashville*

CHRISTIAN SYMBOLISM IN EVANGELICAL CHURCHES

Copyright MCMXLII by Whitmore & Stone

Library of Congress Catalog Number: 42-36418

K

SET UP, PRINTED, AND BOUND BY THE
PARTHENON PRESS, AT NASHVILLE,
TENNESSEE, UNITED STATES OF AMERICA

22999

To the Memory of

My Maternal Grandfather

WILLIAM DALY

1828–1894

Teacher, mathematician, artist—a churchman who
could sincerely say:

"Lord, I have loved the habitation of thy house
And the place where thine honour dwelleth."

Introduction

SYMBOLISM HAS PLAYED a very important part in the proclamation of Christian faith. In the early Church, during the dark centuries of persecution, symbols of the resurrection and the life everlasting helped mightily to maintain morale. In subsequent periods, the Church's teaching and worship inspired the making of other symbols which have served to bring Christian ideas home to the minds and hearts of men. Who possibly could say what the distinctive Christian symbol—the cross—has meant to succeeding generations of Christians?

The need for Christian symbols becomes imperative when, as in our time, the forces of Antichrist undertake to destroy the things for which Jesus stands. "The children of this world look further ahead, in dealing with their own generation, than the children of Light." Indeed, they do when it is they, and not the children of Light, who make emblems that appeal to the imagination and fire the hearts of men.

This book on Christian symbolism is timely. It is distinctive, for it is the first of its kind to be written from the standpoint of Evangelical Christianity. To exact and adequate knowledge there is added here an insight that is able to distinguish between the important and the trivial. There are symbols which have lost their vitality through failure to interpret the best in Christian thought and experience. The symbols which are presented here stand for human ideas and yearnings which are not destined to pass away.

Readers of this book will find delight in the illustrations which the author himself has drawn, and they will be particularly grateful for the definitions of ecclesiastical terms and usages.

ERNEST FREMONT TITTLE

Foreword and Acknowledgments

THERE IS A WIDESPREAD need for an inexpensive and simple treatise on the principal elements of Christian symbolism, written with special regard for the evangelical point of view. This book is an attempt to meet the need.

The subject is of wide scope and cannot be treated exhaustively in limited space. For the most part, in this volume, the author has attempted only to picture and describe the principal symbols which evangelical churches can consistently use—in other words, the symbols which are precious to the various types of Catholics and Evangelicals alike.

By the expression "evangelical churches" is meant the denominational bodies which cling closely to the doctrines derived more or less directly from the New Testament alone, and which accept two sacraments—Holy Communion and Baptism—as symbolical rites rich in spiritual significance.

Furthermore, evangelical bodies are commonly non-liturgical, but this negative term is rather difficult to define. As used in this book, it describes a denomination which is without fixed or elaborate forms of ordinary worship and the worship services of which take only slight account of the Christian Year. However, it should be noted that most of such denominations have a fixed ritual for the administration of Baptism and the Lord's

Supper and for the conduct of customary church ceremonies.

Symbolism in doctrine, ritual and church usage is discussed in this book from the evangelical and non-liturgical standpoint as defined above. However, it should not be inferred from this that the purpose of the book is polemical. It is more nearly correct to say that it is limited in accordance with the title.

Dean Swift, in his famous lampoon, *Gulliver's Travels,* tells of two violently opposed religious sects on the Island of Lilliput; namely, the Big-endians who opened their eggs at the big end, and the Little-endians who strongly preferred the little end—a gibe directed at the extremists of the High Church and the Low Church parties, respectively, leaving the reader to draw the inference that it is the nutritive part of the contents that really matters. Even so!

A few words of heartfelt thanks are due to those friends and helpers whose aid has meant much in the preparation of the manuscript. Although pressed with many duties and the care of a great parish, Dr. Ernest Fremont Tittle very graciously took the time necessary to read it and write the introduction.

For permission to make direct quotations from copyrighted material, I am indebted to Dr. William L. Stidger of Boston University School of Theology; the C. D. Morris Associates, Inc., of New York; The Macmillan Company, New York; Alfred A. Knopf, Inc., New York; Morehouse-Gorham Company, New York; The

American Baptist Publication Society, Philadelphia; E. P. Dutton and Company, New York.

For pictures of churches and other facilities made available, I acknowledge, with gratitude, the help given by Dr. E. M. Conover, Director, Interdenominational Bureau of Architecture, New York City; Edward F. Jansson and Frank L. Venning, Associated Architects, Interdenominational Bureau of Architecture, Chicago; A. F. Wickes, Consulting Architect, Board of Church Extension of the Disciples of Christ, Indianapolis; R. O. Ives, American Seating Company, Chicago; Dr. Boynton Merrill, West Newton, Massachusetts.

I am indebted to the following ministers for their kind co-operation in obtaining the use of pictures of church interiors: the Rev. William R. Shaw, Ypsilanti, Michigan; Dr. Ernest Fremont Tittle, Evanston, Illinois; Dr. Ira G. McCormack, Chicago; the Rev. Edward H. Busekros, Chicago; Dr. Stephen E. Fisher, Champaign, Illinois; Dr. W. Earl Ledden, Albany, New York; the Rev. J. B. Clower, Jr., Virginia Beach, Virginia; Dr. E. M. Jeffords, Wilmette, Illinois.

For the photograph from which the picture, "The Great Chalice of Antioch," was made, and for other courtesies, I am obliged to Mr. Fahim Kouchakji, New York City.

I owe very special thanks to Dr. Arthur Haire Forster, Librarian and Professor of Hellenistic Greek, Seabury-Western Divinity School, Evanston, Illinois, for ready access to the library of that institution, which is well stocked with books on Christian symbolism and

11

related subjects. The Chicago Public Library and the Newberry Library of Chicago have afforded the use of extensive collections of books on symbolism. I am obliged to Dean Ernest Cadman Colwell and Dr. Harold R. Willoughby of The Divinity School, The University of Chicago, for an extensive list of the books on early Christian art and iconography in the library of that institution.

With characteristic catholicity of spirit, Saint Paul declared his indebtedness to Greeks and Barbarians, the wise and unwise. Somewhat in the same vein, I may say that I have consulted with pleasure and profit the works of a good many writers of widely different persuasions regarding doctrine, liturgy and symbolism. The footnotes, throughout the book, bear testimony of indebtedness to this host of scholars in a fascinating field of inquiry and learning.

T. A. S.

Evanston, Illinois

Contents

I

14

Illustrations

15

CHAPTER I

Symbols, Symbolism and Symbolics

THE WORD SYMBOL is derived from two Greek words, *syn*, meaning together, and *ballein*, meaning to throw. Hence, *symbolon*, a sign, mark or token, implying the throwing together or joining of an abstract idea and a visible sign of it; the sign serving to recall it, not by exact resemblance, but by suggestion. Thus a cross is a symbol of Christ's death; a crucifix, which represents the suffering Savior hanging upon a cross, is not a symbol, but is, in effect, a picture.

Christian teaching deals, in part, with supernatural elements which can be vividly suggested to the human mind only by symbolic words and signs. Religion, like life, escapes formulas.

All sensuous things to which a higher meaning, aside from the natural significance, is attributed, are symbols. All religions are measurably symbolic in character. The expression of spiritual truths and abstract notions by analogous phenomena in the physical world has been common to all peoples and religions. To communicate these conceptions to others, and fix them by the laws of association, it is necessary to give them formal expression. Hence, the successful teaching of the doctrines of a religion must in some sense involve symbolism.[1]

In the early Christian Church, symbols were freely used as convenient fixatives of doctrinal points for the

[1] Charles W. Bennett, *Christian Archeology*, Eaton and Mains, 1898, p. 72.

many Christians who could not read and, during periods of persecution, as a secret language. In our day, symbols are used on church windows and furnishings for the purpose of indicating pictographically the cardinal elements of Christian faith, tradition and teaching by presenting to the eye an interesting and valuable supplement to preaching and religious education. When well understood, they are very effective for this purpose and are quite agreeable to our constant use of symbols in everyday life. The familiar act of shaking hands is a symbol of friendship. Saluting the flag of the United States, when it is carried past in procession, is a sign of respect for our country, which is symbolized by "the Stars and Stripes." And so on. While we communicate with each other mostly by speech, nevertheless, we also use a considerable amount of sign language every day, including printed and typewritten matter.

The use of symbolism is intimately connected with the most meaningful and important aspects of the secular social order. It is not to be wondered at when we find similar use profoundly integrated in church life and order. Gazing steadily at a cross, the reverent Christian calls to mind the sufferings of the Divine Savior and the benefits bestowed upon mankind by his passion and death. A cross is the most important of all Christian symbols, because its significance touches us at the greatest depths of our being.

In a certain sense, the great creeds are collections of symbols which do not and cannot compass the complete content of Christian faith. Nobody has ever compiled

18

a creed that can remain unaffected by the passage of time, because the medium of expression is words which, in a living language, are subject to change in meaning and force and, even in a dead language, are not protected against misapprehension in far distant times. Words have in them the inherent limitations of expression characteristic of all symbols. The statements of a creed are suggestive of meaning largely in the same way that pictured symbols are, and it is for this reason that the theological term "Symbolics" is used for the study of creeds and confessions of faith.

In passing, it is interesting to note that in the early Christian church, partly because of the influence of the mystery religions, but mainly for prudential reasons, the creed was regarded as esoteric—not to be revealed to outsiders.

J. R. Lumby, in his *History of the Creeds,* says:

Nothing can be stronger than the language of the Fathers of the Church down to the fifth century on the care with which the creed was to be kept a secret. It was to be preserved in the memory only. The name *Symbolum* is used for it, of which the most probable explanation is that it meant a password whereby Christians recognized each other. Saint Augustine says: "You must not write down anything about the creed, because God said, 'I will put my law in their hearts and in their minds will I write it.' Therefore the creed is learned by hearing and is not written on tablets or any material substance but only in the heart."

It is therefore not surprising that there is no specimen of a creed until the end of the second century, and really the most ancient public written creed is about the end of the third century.[2]

Every evangelical pastor should provide for the instruction of children, not only with regard to the out-

[2] Quoted by P. D. Ouspensky, *A New Model of the Universe,* Alfred A. Knopf, Inc., 1934. Used by permission.

lines of Christian doctrine and history, but also with respect to the great symbols revered by "the holy catholic church" mentioned in the Apostles' Creed and in which evangelical Christians, no less than variously sundered modern Catholics, regularly profess belief. Among other good results, such teaching almost invariably leads to an increase of reverence for "the house of God," surely something to be most earnestly desired. Moreover, the study of Christian symbolism carries one inevitably to the essential roots of the Christian religion, some of which run back interestingly into pre-Christian thought about God and life.[3]

[3] *See* Edwyn R. Bevan, Preface of *Symbolism and Belief,* The Macmillan Co., 1938.

CHAPTER II

The Restoration of Forms and Symbols

SINCE EARLY TIMES, Christian symbolic art and ritual have been very closely connected, a fact which prompted the writing of this preliminary chapter concerning both.[1] During the past quarter century, in the non-liturgical churches in America, there has been manifest a remarkable movement towards the adoption of enriched forms of worship and a more liberal use of symbolical decoration and equipment.

The various Catholic, Episcopal and Lutheran churches are professedly liturgical and make extensive use of the traditional forms and symbolism inherited from the early Christian Church, or developed in the period of magnificent flowering of medieval religious art which preceded the Reformation. During the early stages of the Calvinistic Reformation, much of this heritage was thrown into the discard by wrathful reformers, who wrought havoc on priceless treasures of religious art in Scotland, England and other parts of Europe. Of three hundred sixty Celtic crosses, said to exist in Scotland prior to the Reformation, only two exist today. John Calvin permitted gratification of the ear through poetry and music, but denied gratification of the eye. Genesis

[1] A. G. Hebert, *Liturgy and Society*, Faber and Faber, 1935, pp. 242–250. *See also* Ernest F. Scott, *The Nature of the Early Church*, Scribner's, 1941, pp. 70–95.

21

1:31 was overlooked. In attempting to uproot "super-stitious" and "idolatrous" usages, the Calvinists com-mitted many destructive excesses and, for the sake of stark contrast to Roman Catholic custom, kept their churches almost completely bare of everything that might appeal to the imagination and the esthetic sense of the worshipers. Every candid student of history will admit that they had much provocation. Nevertheless, it now appears that the catharsis was too severe.[2]

The iconoclastic spirit was vigorously expressed among the American pioneers and is not yet moribund. It seems that by many of us the loss of goods by fire may be suffered more easily than the cancelation of in-herited notions and prejudices. Moreover, only the philosophic few believe in a "golden mean." Human beings quite generally tend to indulge in excess, especial-ly in regard to persons and things to which they are opposed. Puritans, like Richard Braithwaite who hanged his cat on Monday because it killed a mouse on Sunday, were capable of great severity in the exercise of what they genuinely conceived to be righteous indignation. Even in our own day genuine piety is sometimes mani-fested in very queer and fanatical forms, and one does not have to be a cynic to observe that the human mind is capable of extraordinary folly with perfect sincerity.

Sometimes the descendants of the early Puritans sought relief from bareness in rather peculiar ways. A short time ago, attracted by its odd-looking exterior, the author visited a certain church, erected about the middle

[2] J. O. Dobson, *Worship*, The Macmillan Co., 1941, p. 75.

of the nineteenth century. To his complete astonishment, he found the interior built and decorated in the style of an ancient Egyptian temple, with symbols and all. The place did not have a single Christian symbol in sight. Oddly enough, the sermon heard in this church was preached on a richly symbolic text found in the Book of Revelation, and during an interesting discourse the preacher made frequent reference to some of the most important early Christian symbols.

Be it noted that this interesting structure belongs to a theologically conservative denomination that is now showing a lively interest in placing altars in its sanctuaries, albeit with due regard for simplicity of effect.

Perhaps a good explanation of the recruiting power of a certain secret society among Protestants in America, for more than a hundred years, has been the richness of its ethical and religious symbolism. Symbolism, banned from the church, flourished in the lodge.

The Lutherans were no less thorough reformers than the Calvinists in purging doctrine of what they regarded as unscriptural and unjustifiable accretions. But in contrast to the Calvinists they retained a considerable degree of respect for venerable ecclesiastical forms and symbols which in their judgment were not inconsistent with the reformed confession of faith. Consequently, all Lutheran bodies have been more or less liturgical from the beginning. For the most part, and in keeping with pioneer simplicity, the earliest Lutheran churches established in America were decidedly plain in appearance. Today, many Lutheran churches are among the finest in the country, and they are usually rich in Christian symbolism, employed with dignity, fitness and restraint.

In regard to ritual, which involves the use of symbolism in a notable degree, it should be mentioned that Archbishop Cranmer (1489-1556), Primate of the Anglican Church, was intimately acquainted with the Lutheran Order of Service. He spent a year and a half in Germany in conference with theologians and liturgical scholars while he was preparing the groundwork of the English *Book of Common Prayer*. Both the Lutheran and the English service books were drawn from the common treasury of the Christian Church of the West, many of the finest collects having been in use for nearly a thousand years when first translated into German and English.

The passage of time has brought the inevitable backward swing of the pendulum from the extreme Calvinistic position regarding forms and symbols, and today we find a considerable number of Presbyterian, Congregationalist, Baptist and Methodist churches introducing enriched forms of worship, altars, crosses, candles, vestments and other ecclesiastical equipment that would have been darkly frowned upon, even as late as the beginning of this century. Apparently a concomitant of all this is a deepening of reverence for the sanctuary as such. In this connection, some interesting cases should be noted: (1) Some time ago an architect noticed several signs, with the word "SILENCE" printed on them in very large type, which were placed around the interior of a very plain and unattractive building called "a church." Needed? Yes! That sort of building invites noise. (2) A Baptist minister, whose people recently built a new church, having a simple but dignified sanctuary with altar and cross, writes: "Our people never tire of the simple, impressive beauty and orderliness of our sanctuary, and almost unanimously have changed from the ordinary whispering Protestant congregation into unusually alert, yet quiet and reverent worshipers." (3) A Methodist pastor reports: "Already there is evidence of the wisdom of the church in making the change. The attendance at the services has almost doubled."

Many churches have found that remodeling, in order to secure such a reverence-producing effect, need not be excessively costly and is likely to be most impressive when kept free of gaudy ornamentation and signs of desire for ritualistic practices foreign to the evangelical conception of worship.

As an indication of the new trend, it is interesting to note that the Rev. George F. Macleod, a well-known minister of the Church of Scotland, and a group of like-minded Scottish ministers and laymen have organized, with at least the tacit consent of the General Assembly of the Church of Scotland, a religious brotherhood known as The Iona Community, the members of which have restored, by the labors of their own hands, a ruined medieval priory and chapel on the sequestered Isle of Iona in western Scotland. Candles are burned on the long neglected Benedictine altar, which now bears a beautiful silver Celtic cross; and a good many devoted men are going there periodically to seek that quiet of mind, discipline of spirit and sense of sanctuary through which the presence of God may be realized without the distractions of which the world is now so full.

It is somewhat difficult today for us to understand how the early Methodists came so soon and so fully under the influence of the Calvinistic attitude with regard to ritual and symbolism, because John and Charles Wesley were both liturgically-minded. John Wesley edited for the use of his followers an excellent abridgment of the Anglican *Book of Common Prayer,* which is notable as much for what he retained as for his excisions. His introduction to that abridgment shows the very high regard he held for the great classic prayer-book which ranks close to the King James Authorized Version of the Bible in beauty of language and persistence of influence. In commending this abridgment to the Methodists in America, he wrote: "I believe there is no liturgy in the world, either in ancient or modern language, which breathes more of a solid, scriptural, rational piety than the Common Prayer of the Church of England. And though the main of it was compiled considerably more than two hundred years ago, yet is the language of it not only pure, but strong and elegant in the highest degree."

For a good many years past, the Wesleyans in England have been using enriched forms of worship, and American Methodism has recently taken long steps in the same direction.

A Free Church Book of Common Prayer, a truly re-markable volume, published anonymously in England in 1929, is indicative of the new trend towards enrichment of the services of worship in English Nonconformist churches. In the introduction, it is declared that the life of the Free Church, "in some of its most distinctive characteristics, derives directly from the New Testa-ment and the earlier practices of the one Catholic Church. Devotionally, their life is coeval with the Christian Faith, and their roots are the same primary roots that feed the life of every Christian communion, ancient or modern, throughout the world." [3]

Inability of this generation to reproduce sincerely many of the spontaneous religious enthusiasms of bygone times compels the search for a norm of divine service that will make worship impressive against a vastly changed scene today. The same ground was traversed with the same result by the Christian Church within the first two centuries of its existence. In an age of diminished controversy, it is now seen that forms and symbols not inconsistent with sound Christian teach-ing are important aids to religious life and thought, if treated meaningfully and reverently.

The language of the Holy Scriptures, in both the Old and the New Testament, is extraordinarily rich in sym-bolism and gives the highest warrant for the use of it. The Bible strongly favors symbolism when legitimately used for instruction, and condemns it when it is con-

[3] *A Free Church Book of Common Prayer,* E. P. Dutton & Co., New York (American publishers), 1929. Used by permission.

verted to idolatrous ends. Such condemnation will always be needed. From the earliest times "Eye-gate" has been an important entrance to the soul of man. Modern psychology has demonstrated that our actions are governed not only by ideas but by that which appeals to the subconscious mind.

At present, the movement towards more liberal use of traditional Christian forms and symbols in Protestant churches is in a somewhat chaotic state. In America, until comparatively recent years, Liturgics and Symbolism have received very limited attention in the training of Protestant ministers, except, of course, in the Protestant Episcopal and the various Lutheran bodies. In a good many theological seminaries, this condition has been changed already and considerable stress is being laid on study of the proper conduct of worship and acquaintance with the historic forms.

Ministers and church officials engaged in remodeling or in building new churches, lacking acquaintance with Christian art, have often permitted architects and artists possessing slight regard for churchly propriety to introduce decorative and symbolic features incongruous with Protestant restraint. Imagine the amusement of certain Roman Catholics upon discovering that a neighboring church of strong Protestant profession had ignorantly selected the Papal Arms for prominent display in a stained glass window! Similar mistakes have been made, although more rarely, by Roman Catholics, as for instance, the incorporation of the Lutheran seal in low relief on an elaborate stone altar.

THE RESTORATION OF FORMS AND SYMBOLS

In building a church, purity of style and sincerity of use, especially in the employment of symbols, will be lightly regarded, unless a churchly-minded architect is consulted. An architect who is unfamiliar with the canons of good form in church building may, in the long run, cause far more expense than a specially trained architect. Besides, he may expose a congregation to ridicule. This statement applies whether the church building is to be large or small, but particularly to the latter. Within the limits of available resources, a properly trained architect will seek to obtain just proportion, sound workmanship and the strength and beauty that inhere in fundamental simplicity and suitability of design. An architect planning a church building without a reverential Christian spirit and an intelligent respect for Christian tradition to guide him in his use of technical knowledge is like an agnostic poet trying to write a hymn—the spirit of the form is not within his ken.

The fault in most of our existing churches today is the lack of dignified and meaningful simplicity. This remark is not made lightly. It is the result of visiting and speaking in hundreds of them from Maine to California. Our aim should be to get rid of the abomination of clutter. It is so unrestful that it is bound to hinder worship.

Because evangelicals are in a transitional stage with respect to ecclesiology, one frequently sees evidences of arrangements and uses that are open to question. For instance, the placement of a cross in the sanctuary floor immediately in front of the altar is inappropriate, because it is at variance with the universally accepted rule of respect which requires that one should not stand or walk on major symbols of the faith.[4] If, when kneeling at the chancel rail for Communion, church members observe the officiating clergyman walking on a cross, the sight will not be inspiring. The flag of our country is our major national symbol, and we would not think of having a copy of it inlaid in the floor of the chancel of a church. But the cross is even more sacred than the flag of our country. Furthermore, it should be noted that a cross placed in the floor of the chancel is out of sight of the members of the congregation, most of whom seldom enter that part of the church. A short time ago, in a beautiful Methodist church recently erected in a Middle Western country town, and modeled after an English parish church, with choir stalls on either side of the approach to the altar, I saw the choirmaster conduct the singing of an anthem by directing the movements of his baton entirely toward the altar and reredos, while standing at a short distance before it. The disconcerting effect of such performance thrust in front of the central objects of interest in the sanctuary can be imagined. A church in an eastern city has a baptismal font held by a large figure of an angel with extended wings, which is placed in the front of the nave of the church so as to obscure, in part, the view of the altar and reredos as one enters the long central aisle. This is an unusual example of bad placement.

In our Protestant churches we are rapidly acquiring

[4] F. R. Webber, *Church Symbolism,* Jansen, Cleveland, 1938, p. 98.

a wealth of venerable forms and symbols, but not always with due concern to possess the understanding spirit which invests them with worth-while significance and impressive sacredness. Employed for the stimulation of faith and reverence, their function is elevating in its effect. Employed as just so much embellishment and garniture, they have the emptiness and futility of creeds much repeated but little believed. "It is at all times better to introduce one symbol with propriety than half a dozen for the sake of ornament." [5] Building altars and putting crosses upon them will not automatically cure fundamental faults in our church life, but whole-hearted acceptance of the spirit of altruistic sacrifice for which the cross stands can rejuvenate the power of the church for good in a pagan world crazed with desire for material things.

There are three virtues worthy of special praise in the use of venerable church forms and symbols; namely, reverence, simplicity and sincerity, not the least of which is sincerity.

[5] W. and G. A. Audsley, *Handbook of Christian Symbolism,* Day & Son, London, 1865, p. 3.

GOD THE FATHER
(PLATE A)

1. HAND OF GOD
(MANUS DEI)

2. SOULS OF THE
RIGHTEOUS

3. HAND OF GOD
(GREEK FORM)

4. YAHWEH

5. THE LORD

6. THE ALMIGHTY

7. YOD IN TRIANGLE

8. ALL-SEEING EYE

9. "I AM THAT I AM"
("ΕΓΟ ΕΙΜΙ Ο ΩΝ")

10. THEOS

32

CHAPTER III

Symbols of the Godhead

I. THE FATHER

THE HAND IS the most ancient symbol of the first Person in the Godhead. The "hand of God" is mentioned in Proverbs [1] and Ecclesiastes.[2] This symbol was employed frequently in early Christian art. It represents the creative power of God. It is often referred to by its Latin name, *Manus Dei,* and sometimes it is called *Dextra Domini* (the right hand of the Lord).[3] The early Christians, like the Hebrews, refrained from representing God in human form.[4] Exodus 33:20 was long regarded as a prohibition against portrayal of God.

Figure A1 is a well-known form of the *Manus Dei* symbol. The hand points downward from a cloud of glory and is surrounded by a nimbus with three rays, known as a tri-radiant nimbus. The use of a tri-radiant nimbus always signifies divinity. The *Manus Dei* is frequently shown with only the thumb and the first two fingers extended in the position of blessing, the third and fourth fingers being closed (see Plate O, Figure 2).

Figure A2 represents the *Manus Dei* as containing five small figures, referring to the famous passage in the Book of Wisdom (Old Testament Apocrypha): "The

[1] 1:24.
[2] 9:1.
[3] Acts 7:55.
[4] Exod. 33:20; John 1:18.

souls of the righteous are in the hand of God." It is also supported by Psalm 139:10.

Figure A3 is a Greek variant of the hand symbol, shown in the attitude of benediction. The first finger is held upright, signifying the letter *I* (Iota); the second finger is bent so as to indicate the letter *C*, which is the early form of the Greek capital letter for *S* (Sigma). The thumb is crossed on the third finger so as to form the letter *X* (Chi), and the little finger is bent so as to indicate the Greek letter *C* (Sigma). *I* and *C* are the first and last letters of the Greek word for Jesus (*Iesous*), and X and C are the first and last letters of the Greek word for Christ (*Xristos*), so that this symbol (A3) signifies the union of God the Father and Jesus Christ his Son.

The Christian symbols for God the Father have their origin in the Old Testament in which various Hebrew names are used for God. The word *Jehovah* is an improper rendering of the Hebrew word *Yahweh*, which signifies: "I am that I am." [5] See Figure A4, in which the word *Yahweh* appears in Hebrew characters. By the Jews this name was considered too sacred to be pronounced, even in the sacred precincts of the Temple. [6] Another Hebrew name for God is *Adonai* (the Lord), the Hebrew characters for which are shown in Figure A5. This word was a term of respect used for a superior person and its common use corresponded with the Eng-

[5] Exod. 3:14.

[6] Similarly, out of reverence, the Egyptians addressed their ruler by the title *Pero*, meaning "the great house," his particular name being regarded as too sacred to be spoken. *Pharaoh* is the Hebrew form of *Pero*.

lish mode of address, "My Lord," used in addressing nobility. In its highest sense *Adonai* was sometimes used as a prefix to Yahweh.[7] *El Shaddai*, meaning "the Almighty," was a primitive name for divinity and was retained in use among the Hebrews after their concept of God had been refined by Mosaic teaching. It is shown in Figure A6, the characters being read from right to left in the Hebrew language. *Adonai* and *El Shaddai* were used as substitutes for the name *Yahweh*, which was forbidden to be uttered. The rays of light surrounding the three most important Hebrew names for the Divine Being indicate glory.

God is often represented in Christian art by the Hebrew letter *Yod* enclosed in an equilateral triangle. *Yod* is the first letter of the word *Yahweh*. The triangle with three equal sides is used to represent the Holy Trinity. (See Figure A7.)

A very stern symbol of God the Father is the All-seeing Eye, ecclesiastical use of which originated in the sixteenth century (see Figure A8). It was frequently used in Great Britain, in the days of long sermons, and was usually placed on the wall, directly behind the pulpit, with a view to making the preached word and the omniscience of God impressive. It is the emblem of Deity in the lodges of a leading secret society.[8] As a symbol of the power, majesty and omnipresence of God, it is appropriate in a church window above an altar.

[7] Gen. 15:2; Deut. 3:24.

[8] The origin of this symbol is connected with sun-worship. William Tyler Olcott, *Sun Lore of All Ages*, Putnam's, 1914, p. 302.

Figure A9 shows a Greek form of the Hebrew expression, "I am that I am." The last two Greek words are placed in the circle of rays and made to stand for the whole expression which is shown in Greek capitals directly beneath the English title under Figure A9.

In Christian art, God is represented sometimes by the first and last letters of the Greek equivalent word, *Theos*, with a contraction mark placed above them (see Figure A10).

II. THE SON

In the catacombs of Rome, and other ancient Italian cities, some of the earliest symbols of our Lord may be found. These underground passages contain a vast number of niches which were used as burial vaults.[1] On the slabs of stone or marble used to seal the niches containing the remains of Christians, it was customary to place Christian symbols and inscriptions. Some of these symbols belong to the first century.

The fish is one of the earliest and most complex symbols employed by Christians to represent the Savior (see Figure B1). Clement of Alexandria (A.D. 150–220) mentions and recommends the use of this symbol but does not explain its significance, a fact which indicates that it was commonly understood in his time. Reading the initials of the Greek acrostic phrase, meaning "Jesus

[1] Wonderful representations of portions of the Roman catacombs may be seen in a specially constructed underground museum in Montreal, Quebec. There is a somewhat similar museum in a suburb of Washington, D. C.

GOD THE SON
(PLATE B)

IXΘYC

1. THE FISH

2. VESICA

3. LIGHT OF THE WORLD

4. PELICAN-IN-HER-PIETY

5. THE GOOD SHEPHERD

6. THE SUN OF RIGHTEOUSNESS

7. KING OF KINGS

8. AGNUS DEI AND BOOK OF 7 SEALS

9. AGNUS DEI AND BANNER

37

Christ, Son of God, Savior," one obtains the Greek word for "fish," *Ichthus*,[2] as shown below:

THE GREEK ACROSTIC PHRASE	TRANSLITERATION	LITERAL TRANSLATION	THE SYMBOLIC WORD [3]
Ἰησοῦς	*Iesous*	Jesus	I = i
Χριστὸς	*Christos*	Christ	X = ch
Θεοῦ	*Theou*	of God	Θ = th
Τἱὸς	*Huios*	Son	Τ = u
Σωτήρ	*Soter*	Savior	Σ = s

The fish symbol was probably used by the persecuted Christians as a means of avoiding unpleasant attention of the Roman police. When displayed outside a pagan home, it indicated that a funeral banquet was being held for the dead, but when it appeared outside a Christian home, it was a sign that the Lord's Supper would be celebrated there, at night, in secret.[4]

Alice M. Brookman, in *"My Own" Workbook on Christian Symbolism*, describes effectively the manner in which this symbolic word was used among slaves:

A young Greek slave was on an errand in the home of his master's friend in the city of Rome. He gave his message to the mis-

---

[2] Approximate Anglicized pronounciation, *ick-thees* (s as in "atlas).

[3] Mrs. Jameson, in *Sacred and Legendary Art*, I, 28, states that "the five Greek letters, which express the word fish, form the anagram of the name of Jesus Christ." However, an anagram is a word or phrase obtained by reversing the order of the letters in another word or phrase; *e.g.*, *evil* is an anagram of *live*. There is no anagram in Greek for *Ichthus*. Other authors sometimes refer to the word *Ichthus* as a rebus. A rebus is a picture puzzle in which words, phrases or sentences are represented by pictures. Rebus can be applied to the picture of a fish, but not properly to the word for fish. The use of a picture of a fish as a symbol of Jesus Christ antedated the invention of the acrostic phrase given above.

[4] For full discussion of the various meanings attached to this symbol in the early centuries, *see* Charles W. Bennett, *Christian Archeology*, Eaton and Mains, New York, 1898.

tress of the house, who was seated with her maidens in the court. As he turned to leave, he caught the eye of one of the slave girls, a Greek like himself, and said, "Ichthus?" She flushed, clasped her hands and said with a glad smile, "Ichthus!" The mistress saw, heard and frowningly bade the girl go on with her embroidery. But she thought to herself, "What could that word have meant that it could bring that happy smile?" and on her husband's return she asked him what "ichthus" meant. "It means 'fish,' my dear," he responded. More puzzled than ever, she said to the maid, "What does 'ichthus' mean?" "Madam, it means 'fish,'" replied the maid. To the mistress all the word meant was "fish," but to these two young people, strangers and slaves, it meant "We're both Christians. This is our password. We both love our Lord Jesus Christ."[5]

The fish symbol was used in a great many ways on murals and engravings. Small images of it were made in wood or stone and carried by the Christians as means of identification. These images were sometimes inscribed with the Greek word *Soseis,* meaning "you will save."

Tertullian, in his treatise on baptism, linking the symbol of salvation (a fish) and the symbol of baptismal rebirth (water), says, "We are little fish, and like our Fish, Jesus Christ, we are born in the water, and we are not safe in any other way than by remaining in the water." The little fish, of course, represent symbolically the souls which presumably have become Christlike through baptism.

It is a curious fact that the *Ichthus* symbol came into use in the Latin Church, but it is not included in the

[5] Used by permission of Morehouse-Gorham Co., New York.

symbols used by the Greek Church. The pagan Greeks often carved the figure of a fish on tombs, because they believed that a fish or dolphin carried the soul of the deceased to the isles of the blest. The early Christians ate roasted fish in commemoration of Christ's Passion, and the present-day Roman Catholic custom of eating fish on Good Friday is a survival of this ceremony.

Closely related to the fish symbol, and more common in modern Christian art, is the *vesica piscis* symbol, so named because of supposed resemblance to the bladder of a fish (see Figure B2). It is commonly regarded as a conventionalized form of a fish and is frequently used as an elongated nimbus, usually surrounded by rays, to enclose the figure of the Savior. In this form it is known as the *vesica piscis aureole*.

Upon every Christian altar there should stand at least two candles, set in candlesticks, one on each side of the cross. When lighted, they proclaim our Lord's words, "I am the light of the world" [6] (see Figure B3). When two candles stand on the altar, they symbolize our Lord's twofold nature—human and divine.

The so-called "Pelican-in-her-Piety" (see Figure B4) is a very interesting Christian symbol of the Atonement. It was much used in medieval times and appears in a good many Christian churches in our own day. It is mentioned by Saint Augustine and other early Christian writers. It was believed that the pelican, during times when food was scarce, tore a hole in her breast and fed her young with her blood. This obvious fable may have

[6] John 8:12.

had its origin in the fact that the pelican opens her bill and the young ones reach into her mouth in order that they may get the supply of food in the large pouch beneath the lower half of her beak. Probably the origin of the symbol is in an early Christian book, the *Physiologus*, which describes animals, some of them imaginary, others real, but with more or less imaginary habits. In the noble Eucharistic hymn of Saint Thomas Aquinas, in Latin, known as *"Adoro Te Devote,"* Christ is referred to under this figure:

> *"O loving Pelican! O Jesu Lord!*
> *Unclean I am, but cleanse me in Thy Blood!"*

The symbol known as "The Good Shepherd" is based on John 10:11 (see Figure B5). In the earliest examples, the Shepherd is shown as a young man carrying a sheep on his shoulder, as is customary in Palestine and Syria. The traditional figure is sturdy, indicating the ability of the Shepherd to defend his sheep.[7] In connection with the symbol of "The Good Shepherd," it should be mentioned that the early Christians, under influence of the Greek classics, sometimes used a picture of Orpheus as a type of Christ, because it was believed that Orpheus with his lyre could tame wild beasts. This figure was employed to represent the power of Christ to tame the wild passions of sinful men. The figure of Christ, in such representations, showed him with his lyre surrounded by tamed beasts made mild by his charms.

[7] Ps. 23:4.

41

The sun is a Messianic symbol of Christ. This symbol is probably based on "But unto you that fear my name shall the sun of righteousness arise with healing in its wings."[8] In Figure B6, the monogram represents the first three letters of the word "Jesus" in Greek. However, the form of the letters, as shown, is Gothic. Later, in this book, a full explanation of this important monogram is given. The circle surrounding the monogram represents eternity. The rays, which are alternately straight and wavy, indicate glory.

Prominent among fabled animals, used as symbols of Christ, is the unicorn. A certain kind of antelope, when seen in profile, appears to have only one horn. Lacking the caution of the modern scientific mind, the ancients gave free rein to imagination. We should not condemn them too severely for this, for strange monsters have been reported from the Scottish Loch Ness and elsewhere in our own day. The ancients believed that the unicorn was so elusive that it could be captured only by secluding in a forest a virgin to whom it would run and place its head upon her knees. This belief led to the use of the unicorn as a symbol of the virgin birth of our Lord.

A crown is used as a symbol of the kingly office of Christ (see Figure B7). "For he is Lord of lords and King of kings."[9] "And he hath on his garment and on his thigh a name written, KING OF KINGS, AND LORD OF LORDS."[10] "The crown of life" is a sym-

[8] Mal. 4:2.
[9] Rev. 17:14.
[10] Rev. 19:16.

bolical expression derived from Revelation 2:10 and 3:
11, referring to eternal life through our Lord Jesus
Christ.

"The Lamb of God" (Latin, *Agnus Dei*) is a symbolical title of very ancient origin.[11] In early examples
the *Agnus Dei* symbol appears in two forms (see Figures
B8 and B9). In the first, the Lamb is seen lying upon
the Book of Seven Seals,[12] and in the second, the Lamb
carries the Banner of Victory. Sometimes the Lamb is
shown reclining and holding a banner. The significance
of this form is suffering rather than triumph. The head
is always shown surrounded with a three-rayed nimbus,
significant of divinity. This is one of the most beautiful
of all ancient symbols of our Lord. It is common in the
Roman catacombs. The banner, often called the Easter
or Resurrection banner, symbolizes Christ's victory over
death. When shown in color, it is a white pennant bearing a red cross. A white pennant was sometimes used
as a symbol of Christ's body. In Figure B9 we see the
white pennant, representing Christ's body, attached to
the cruciform staff, thereby signifying his death on
the cross. The risen and triumphant Lamb of God is
portrayed as bearing the emblem of his victory over
death. Perhaps this is the greatest of all symbols used in
Christian art to represent the Son of God.

III. THE HOLY SPIRIT

The most used and most authentic symbol of the
Holy Spirit is the descending dove with the tri-radiant

[11] Isa. 53:7; John 1:29; Rev. 5:12.
[12] Rev. 5:1.

43

GOD THE HOLY SPIRIT
(PLATE C)

1. DESCENDING DOVE

2. SEVEN-TONGUED FLAME

5. SEVEN DOVES

3. THE SEVEN LAMPS

4. MENORAH
SEVEN-BRANCHED CANDLESTICK

44

nimbus (see Figure C1). It is based on the account of the baptism of our Lord.[1] This is one of the earliest forms used to represent the Holy Spirit and is the most beautiful of all the symbols used in Christian art. It is the preferred symbol for baptismal fonts.

The Holy Spirit is sometimes represented indirectly as a cloven flame of fire, or as seven flames (see Figure C2). This symbol is based on the story of Pentecost contained in the second chapter of Acts.

The seven lamps, referred to in Revelation 4:5, have also been used as symbolic of the Holy Spirit (see Figure C3). Traditionally, the seven gifts of the Holy Spirit as taken from Revelation 5:12 are: Power, Riches, Wisdom, Strength, Honour, Glory and Blessing. They are sometimes represented by a seven-branched candlestick, called a Menorah (see Figure C4).

In Figure C5, the seven gifts of the Holy Spirit are represented by seven doves surrounding a circle, in which is inscribed the letters SS, an abbreviation of *Sanctus Spiritus* (Latin for Holy Spirit). In somewhat different form, this beautiful device is used in the ceiling of the Chapel of the Holy Spirit, the Episcopal Cathedral, Washington, D. C.[2]

Sometimes the list of gifts of the Holy Spirit contained in Isaiah, chap. 11, is preferred, although verse two of that chapter mentions only six while the seventh must be construed from the verses following.

---

[1] Matt. 3:16; Mark 1:10; Luke 3:22; John 1:32.

[2] This cathedral is a vast treasure house of extraordinarily fine examples of Christian art. A visit to it will delight the eye, educate the mind and refresh the spirit.

Pope Urban VIII, in A.D. 1623, forbade the use of pictures of the human form to represent the Holy Spirit, and this wise prohibition has been effective since.

Rather rarely the Holy Spirit has been symbolized by an eagle, but this is not favored, because traditionally the eagle has been reserved for representation of Saint John, the commonly accepted author of the fourth Gospel.

IV. THE HOLY TRINITY

The belief in a Triune God is a basic element of Christian faith and teaching. Early in the life of the Christian Church, the doctrine of the Trinity became a storm-center of prolonged and sometimes very bitter controversy. Many definite statements concerning this doctrine are found in the writings of Gregory (Thaumaturgus), Tertullian and other patristic controversialists. Theological debate on the subject continued with varying intensity, from the third to the seventh century, often engaged in by men of first-rate intellectual powers.

The Athanasian Creed, in its first Article, sets forth the doctrine with great elaboration: "We worship One God in Trinity, and Trinity in Unity; neither confounding the Persons, nor dividing the Substance. For there is One Person of the FATHER, another of the SON, and another of the HOLY GHOST. . . . . The Father is GOD, the SON is GOD, and the HOLY GHOST is GOD; and yet there are not three GODS, but one GOD, ..." et cetera.

In our own day, a theologian, with a flair for employing science in the explanation of this doctrine, has writ-

46

ten a book in which he seeks to prove that Threeness and Togetherness are attributes of the Space-Time-Matter structure of the universe, as well as of its Creator. He points out that Space is composed of three essential and mutually dependent dimensions: length, breadth and height (arguing that "the fourth dimension," so-called, is functional rather than dimensional). Furthermore, he states that Time is divisible into three interdependent phases: future, present, past—the present flowing momentarily out of the future into the past.[1]

Matter has three phases; namely, energy, motion and phenomena resulting from latent energy set in motion. Within Space, Time and Matter, respectively, the three essential constituent elements of each are mutually dependent. Likewise, Space, Time and Matter are interdependent, and they must be conjoined in order to produce the universe. (The interrelationship mentioned pertains to the basic structure of the universe only.) Hence, he finds support for the reasonableness of belief in the character of the Divine Trinity as expressed in the great Christian Creeds.[2] If one is not content to let this complex doctrine rest entirely in the realm of mystery, he may find help in this view of the architecture of the universe as a reflection of the nature of its Creator.

It used to be a favorite argument of deists that the doctrine of the Trinity is a mathematical absurdity, be-

---

[1] For a philosophic discussion of Time, see Edwyn R. Bevan, *Symbolism and Belief*, The Macmillan Co., 1938, chap. 4.

[2] Nathan R. Wood, *The Secret of the Universe*, The Warwick Press, Boston, 1936.

cause $1+1+1 = 3$ always and everywhere. This argument can be disposed of mathematically. Persons familiar with the important mathematical laws of probability know that $1\times1\times1 = 1$, when three equal and mutually dependent forces, factors or contingencies are *operating together,* because the value of their joint action is obtained by multiplication rather than by addition. According to the Christian doctrine, the three co-ordinate Persons in the Trinity always operate together in perfect community of thought, purpose and action and, for what it is worth, the aforementioned mathematical law of probability is given as an additional aid in considering the reasonableness of this great fundamental tenet of Christian faith. Of course, as Edwyn Bevan says in *Symbolism and Belief,* "it is only in the sense of giving rational comfort to people who already believe in God that the standard arguments can be regarded as demonstrating the existence of God." [3] Likewise, the doctrine of the Trinity. Such arguments seldom convince confirmed unbelievers. They are interesting mainly to those who have "the will to believe."

In view of the importance of the doctrine of the Holy Trinity and the prolonged controversial struggle concerning it in the early Christian Church, it is surprising to learn that no early symbol for it has been discovered. Such symbols as we possess had their origin mostly in medieval or modern times, and nearly all are geometrical forms intended to explain the nature of three-in-one-

Gifford Lectures, 1933-34, University of Edinburgh, The Macmillan Co., New York, 1938, p. 386. Used by permission.

ness. In most cases, therefore, their import is more on the mathematical than the theological side.

In the figure enclosed at the top of Plate D, we have a copy of an interesting shield designed in the sixteenth century. It is sometimes referred to as the *Scutum Fidei,* or "Shield of Faith." Strictly regarded, it is not a symbol, but rather an ingenious means of expressing the theological import of the doctrine of the Trinity. The circle in the center bears the word *Deus* (Latin, God), while the three other circles are designated in Latin for the Father, the Son and the Holy Spirit, respectively, the words for the Holy Spirit being abbreviated. Each outer circle is joined to the center circle by the Latin word for "is" (*est*), so that one may read, "the Father (*Pater*) is God, the Son (*Filius*) is God, the Holy Spirit (*Spiritus Sanctus*) is God." The outer circles are joined by the Latin words for "is not" (*non est*), so that one may read, "the Father is not the Holy Spirit, etc." This shield may be read in any direction without confusion of meaning.

Perhaps the most commonly used symbol of the Holy Trinity is an equilateral triangle (see Figure D1). It reminds us that the three Persons are "co-equal," as stated in the Athanasian Creed. A beautiful variant of the triangle is shown in Figure D9. It is based on Isaiah 6:3. An ambivalent symbol, used for the Trinity, is the double triangle (see Figure D2). In Christian usage, it is merely an elaboration of Figure D1. In Jewish usage, this symbol is nearly always found in the decoration of modern temples, and is variously called "the Star of

49

David," "the Shield of David," and "Solomon's Seal."
It is used on the Zionist flag in Palestine and elsewhere.
According to tradition, David's shield was of this
shape, and Solomon is said to have worked miracles with
a hexagram. Nothing is certainly known of its origin
as a Jewish symbol, and it was not used as such prior
to the third century A.D. No reference is made to it in
the Old Testament. There is reason for believing that
it had its origin in primitive veneration of the generative
principle in nature, the oppositely placed triangles representing male and female. As a six-pointed star, it is
discussed in the chapter on "Symbolic Stars." [4] Figure
D3 shows the equilateral triangle enclosed within a
circle, and Figure D4 is a more elaborate variant of these
two symbols in combination, the circle signifying the
eternal duration of the Trinity.

Figure D5 is known as the trefoil, which is a familiar
emblem of the Trinity in modern Christian churches.
It is really a modification of the three circles of equal
size, with the overlapping parts cut out (see Figure
D10). In Figure D5 the three lobes are of equal size
and sometimes this device is modified, as in Figure D8,
by inserting three angles between the three lobes. Figure
D6 is called a triquetra and is one of the most beautiful
and most satisfying of the symbols of the Holy Trinity.
The three equal arcs of the circle denote equality of the
three Persons of the Godhead. The lines run continuously and therefore express their eternal existence. They
are interwoven, which expresses their unity. The cen-

[4] See page 83.

THE HOLY TRINITY
(PLATE D)

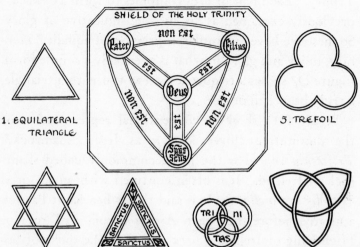

SHIELD OF THE HOLY TRINITY

1. EQUILATERAL
   TRIANGLE

5. TREFOIL

2. TWO TRIANGLES   9." HOLY-HOLY-HOLY"   10. THREE CIRCLES   6. TRIQUETRA

3. TRIANGLE IN
   CIRCLE

11. ST. PATRICK'S
    SHAMROCK

7. TRIQUETRA
   AND TRIANGLE

4. CIRCLE IN TRIANGLE   12. FLEUR-DE-LYS

8. TREFOIL WITH
   POINTS

ter forms an equilateral triangle, itself a symbol of the Trinity. Each pair of arcs combines to form a "vesica," previously explained as an aureole, indicative of glory. So, here we have a complex expression of equality, eternity, unity and glory in what is essentially a simple form. Figure D7 shows a triquetra interwoven with a triangle, a truly beautiful device.

Figure D11 shows a conventional representation of the diminutive clover known as Irish "shamrock." *Trifolium repens* is the plant commonly called shamrock in Ireland. It is often confused with wood-sorrel (*Oxalis acetosella*).[5] It is said that when Saint Patrick appeared before the pagan *Ard-ri* (pron. Ard'-ree) or High King of Ireland (*circa* A.D. 464), he spoke of belief in the Holy Trinity. The astonished monarch was angry, because the idea that three Persons could exist as One seemed absurd to him. As the story runs, Saint Patrick stooped, lifted a sprig of shamrock from the grass and, presenting it to the king said: "Here is a perfect leaf with three perfect parts." At first, the king frowned, then, when the idea suddenly dawned on him, he smiled acceptance. So goes one version of the legendary tale, which, whether true or not, has caused this little plant to be one of the best known symbols of the Holy Trinity.

Figure D12, known as the Fleur-de-Lys [6] (French: "flower of the lily") is the iris, which is used to represent

[5] L. H. Bailey, *Standard Encyclopedia of Horticulture*, The Macmillan Co., 1935.

[6] Fleur-de-Lys is the singular form. Two or more of these figures are referred to as Fleur-de-Lis.

the purity of the Virgin Mary, as well as to symbolize the Holy Trinity. In heraldry, it was the emblem of the former royal family of France, a use probably derived from ecclesiastical art. It should be noted that Figure D12 symbolizes threeness in the "standards," in the bands below them, in the "falls" below the bands, and in the anthers. Of course, this is a purely conventional treatment of the flower. However, it is very effective for the purpose intended.

One frequently sees in modern church carvings and sometimes in stained glass church windows, three fish placed so as to form roughly a triangle. Christians were anciently thought of as fish gathered in the net of the Church and, as fish are born in the water, so symbolically speaking, Christians were regarded as "born again" in the water. Three fish arranged approximately in the form of a triangle, on a baptismal font, signify that Christians are baptized "in the Name of the Father, and of the Son, and of the Holy Spirit." One fish alone symbolizes the Second Person of the Trinity; three fish symbolize the three Persons, the latter usage being probably based in part on the fifth chapter of the first epistle of John, and perhaps also, to some extent, on the third chapter of John's Gospel, in which it is taught that the Father and the Son and the Holy Spirit co-operate in man's salvation.

SACRED MONOGRAMS
(PLATE E)

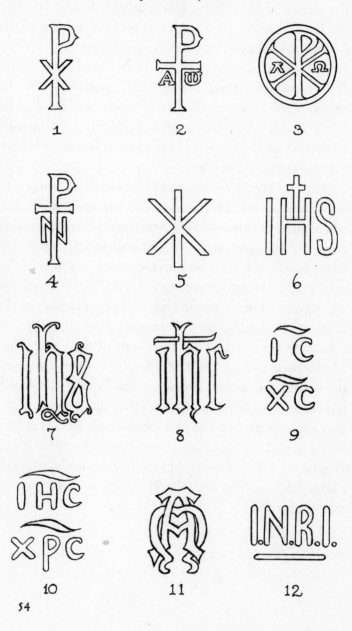

CHAPTER IV

Sacred Monograms

THE USE OF monograms to represent Jesus Christ our Lord is of very early origin. Strictly speaking, these monograms are not symbolic, although they are commonly referred to as symbols. Some of them will be found very frequently in association with well-known symbols of Christ, and therefore a working acquaintance with them is necessary to the understanding of Christian art.

Figure E1 is known as the "Chi Rho" (usually pronounced *Ky Ro*). It is the oldest monogram used with reference to Christ and is sometimes called a "Christogram." The word "Christ," when spelled in ancient Greek capital letters took the form *XPICTOC;* the uncial form of S (Sigma) being like the Roman capital C. The whole word is represented by the first two letters *XP,* which are called "Chi Rho," and have approximately the phonetic effect of English *KR.* The device in Figure E1 is obtained by combining these two letters, the second letter being much larger than the first for the sake of effect.

Christianity's first imperial convert, the wily and ingenious Constantine the Great (A.D. 274–337), probably used this sign ambiguously on the "labarum" or banner carried by the Roman cavalry. See accompanying illustration. It was a clever adaptation of an old Roman ensign. bearing portraits of the Emperor and his sons, with the "XP" monogram mounted at the top and intended to represent the first two letters of the Greek word *XPECTOC*,[1] probably meaning "good" omen when carried in battle. Few of the soldiers were able to read Greek, so the monogram could be interpreted to Christian legionaries as referring to Christ, while pagans interpreted it quite otherwise.[2] The story of the apparition of the "XP" sign in the sky and the inspiration it gave to the Christian soldiers before the battle in which Constantine defeated Maxentius at the Mulvian Bridge in the city of Rome (A.D. 312) is widely known.[3] This victory was the immediate occasion for issuance by Constantine of the Edict of Toleration for Christians, an event which radically changed the course of both Roman and Christian history.

"EN TOYTΩ NIKA"
"IN HOC SIGNO VINCES"
LABARUM OF CONSTANTINE

Figure E2 shows the Christogram in combination with the first and last letters of the Greek

---

[1] This word, used as a given name, meant, "good," whereas, the word *XPICTOC* meant "smeared" or "anointed." Edwyn Bevan, *Christianity*, Home University Library, London; Henry Holt and Co., 1935.

[2] Bertha Diener, *Imperial Byzantium*, Little Brown and Co., 1938, p. 33.

[3] According to legend, the symbol appeared with words underneath, meaning "In this sign thou shalt conquer" (*in hoc signo vinces*).

alphabet, Alpha and Omega; the Omega being in the minuscule (small letter) form in this case. This usage is based on Revelation 22:13, "I am the Alpha and the Omega, the first and the last, the beginning and the end." The letter *X* is read by turning the figure around until the crossed arms appear like *X*. Looked at in the perpendicular position, it suggests a cross.

Figure E3 is another form in which the letters are enclosed in a circle to indicate the eternal existence of the second Person in the Godhead. Note that Omega is in the majuscule (capital) form in this case. This beautiful device appears frequently in modern Christian art. It signifies that the eternal Christ is the beginning and end of all things.

Figure E4 contains the Greek letter *N* for *NIKA*, which means "Victor," and the monogram should be interpreted "Christ the Victor" (*Christus Victor*).

Figure E5 is a combination of the first letter of the Greek word for Jesus (*IHCOUC*) and the first letter of the word for Christ (*XPICTOC*).

Figure E6 is a modernized form of *IHC*, the first three letters of the Greek word for Jesus, with a cross inserted above the horizontal part of the letter *H*. A glance at the vinculum (contraction sign) which appears in Figure E8 gives a clue to the probable origin of this use of the cross, which is not objectionable. It must not be forgotten that the English equivalent of the Greek capital *H* is *E*, and that *C* is an old form of the Greek capital letter S (Sigma). There is no letter *J* in the Greek alphabet, hence the use of *I*.

In Figure E7, we have a Gothic form of *IHC* which came into use in the Middle Ages when Greek was not understood by priests and monks. Because of this, it was variously interpreted, and it is believed that a Franciscan monk, Saint Bernardine of Siena (A.D. 1380–1444), was responsible for the unauthentic interpretation, *"Jesus Hominum Salvator"* (Jesus the Savior of Mankind).[4] This interpretation is given very frequently today, but it is totally without foundation. These letters have only one true significance; namely, they are the three first letters of the word Jesus written in Greek capitals. All dependable authorities agree on this point.

Figure E8 is a modification of E7 in the direction of restoring the earlier form of the letter *Sigma*. The use of E8 in preference to E7 is favored by those who wish to emphasize the Greek origin of the monogram. It has an interwoven bar, or vinculum, indicating contraction. The Gothic letter *h* takes the place of the Greek *H*. The mistaking of the Greek capital letter *Eta* for *h* in the Middle Ages by monastic scribes, unfamiliar with classical languages, led to the kind of misinterpretation already mentioned. The minuscule form of *Eta* is η,

[4]Other interpretations may be heard, among them the following:

> English: I have suffered;
> German: *Jesus, Heiland, Seligmacher;*
> Latin: *In hoc signo (vinces);*
> Greek: *Iesous, Hiereus, Soter.*

"Jesus Christ the Saviour of Mankind" is an obvious hybrid, the result of confusing the meaning of *Ichthus* with *Jesus Hominum Salvator.*

In one of the parishes of the Episcopalian Diocese of Clogher, Northern Ireland, a lady named Isabel Harriett Strong presented to the parish church an altar cloth with the monogram *IHS* embroidered on it. Shortly afterwards, a woman of the parish, on seeing it, ignorantly remarked: "She thought well enough of herself to put her initials on it!"

which probably had something to do with the transformation.

In Figure E9, we have the first and last letters, respectively, of the Greek words for Jesus Christ, with contraction signs above each. Figure E10 uses the Greek letters *IHC* and *XPC* (with contraction signs above them) to represent "Jesus Christ."

Figure E11 is an elaborate form of *Alpha-Omega*. It should be noted here that it is improper to use these letters alone. They should always be used in connection with a monogram or symbol signifying Jesus Christ; otherwise, their meaning would be merely two letters of the Greek alphabet. One sees examples of this misuse in many churches. It should be noted also that it is quite improper to use the letters *IHC* or *IHS* with points inserted between them. *I.H.S.* is an inexcusable form which alas! one sees occasionally. *J.H.S.* is worse, because the letter I is the first letter of the word for Jesus in both its Latin and Greek forms.

In Figure E12, the Roman letters *I.N.R.I.* stand for the Latin words *Iesus Nazarenus Rex Iudaeorum* (Jesus of Nazareth, the King of the Jews). This was the superscription placed by order of Pontius Pilate, in Greek, Latin and Hebrew, on the upper part of the cross on which our Lord was crucified. Note that the points between the letters are perfectly proper in Figure E12.

In the decoration and furnishings of a church, the pastor and the committee in charge of property should take pains to ensure that the use of any of the aforementioned sacred monograms shall be made only after careful study of setting and significance.

CHAPTER V

Symbols of Christ's Suffering

I. HIS PASSION AND DEATH

INCREASINGLY, EVANGELICAL CHURCHES are placing
emphasis on proper observation of the Lenten period in
the Christian Year. Nowadays, in many of them, the
special services of this period are the only reminder of
the annual period of "revival" which used to be so common in the days of our youth.

The Lenten period is usually chosen as the time when
young persons undergo training preparatory to reception into full membership in the church. This period
is therefore an excellent time during which the pastor
can open to both probationers and membership the rich
treasuries of Christian symbolism.

As most churches are equipped with a stereopticon,
there ought to be made available a set of lantern slides
covering the principal Christian symbols, with a brief
accompanying lecture, the text of which could be sup-
plemented by explanations given by the pastor. If such
sets were made available, most churches could afford to
buy one and keep it permanently for annual use during
Lent or some other suitable time during the Christian
Year.

In Plate F there are twelve drawings of symbols connected with the passion, death and resurrection of our

Lord. In the interest of completeness five more should be added. They will be described at the end of this chapter.

Figure F1, a chalice and a cross, represents the agony of Christ in the Garden of Gethsemane. The cross in this case is known as "the Cross of Suffering," or "the Cross of Agony," and is distinguished by the pointed ends.[1] This striking symbol may be seen frequently in stained glass windows.

The lantern pictured in Figure F2 is a symbol of the betrayal. The proper reference is John 18:3 from which, also, symbol F3 is derived.

Figure F4—the sword and staff. This is another symbol of the betrayal based on the Scripture story, as is Figure F5, which shows the purse and thirty pieces of silver—the price of Judas' perfidy.[2]

In Figure F6, we have a representation of Peter's sword and the severed ear of Malchus, reminding us of an important incident which occurred at the arrest of Jesus.[3]

Two scourges arranged in saltier (crossed like an X) against a whipping post are shown in Figure F7. This symbol is based on Matthew 27:26 and Mark 15:15.

Figure F8 depicts the crown of thorns interwoven about three nails, symbolizing the torture and crucifixion of our Lord. Frequently the three nails are used separately as a symbol of the crucifixion. Sometimes the initials *I.N.R.I.* are inserted in the space enclosed by the

[1] Luke 22:42.
[2] Matt. 26:15.
[3] Luke 22:50-51; John 18:10-11.

CHRIST'S PASSION, DEATH AND RESURRECTION
(PLATE F)

1 GETHSEMANE

2. LANTERN

3. TORCH

4. SWORD AND STAFF

5. BETRAYAL

6. SWORD AND EAR

7. SCOURGES

8. CROWN OF THORNS AND NAILS

9. SEAMLESS ROBE

10. LADDER, REED AND SPONGE

11. CRUCIFIXION

12. RESURRECTION

thorns. These initials have been explained in the previous chapter.

Figure F9 symbolizes our Lord's seamless robe or
tunic, for possession of which the Roman soldiers cast
lots, the lottery being indicated by three dice.[4]

Figure F10, a reed and a sponge arranged across a
ladder in saltier, may be seen quite frequently as a symbol of the crucifixion.[5] Usually the length of the ladder
is exaggerated, as the crosses generally used by the Ro-
mans did not rise high above the ground.

Figure F11 represents the crucified Christ upon the
cross, with Pilate's superscription on the upper part;
and Figure F12 shows the empty cross and the distant
rising sun of the Resurrection Morn.

In addition to the symbols already described, there are
several others which should be mentioned and described
briefly:

a) A picture of a rope signifying the binding of
Christ, before he was led into the presence of Annas
and thence to Caiaphas, is frequently found among
symbols of the passion.[6]

b) A basin with a pitcher, or ewer, above it signifies
the washing of Pilate's hands to declare his belief in the
innocence of Jesus. Among modern Christians, nobody
ever speaks a good word for Pilate who, unwillingly,
condemned Jesus to death on a political charge which
was unsupported by evidence; but apparently this was

[4] Matt. 27:25; John 19:23.
[5] Matt. 27:48.
[6] John 18:12.

not uniformly the view of the early Christians, some of whom regarded Pilate leniently.

c) A cock in the act of crowing is frequently employed as a symbol of Peter's denial.[7] (See also Plate N, which contains several symbols of Christ's passion and death, supplementary to those shown in Plate F.)

d) Sometimes one sees a picture of a reed with a bundle of hyssop affixed on the end and a bowl underneath. The hyssop is mentioned in John 19:29. A reed and hyssop were used by the Jews in a rite symbolizing purgation or cleansing.[8] It has been conjectured that the Roman soldiers dipped a branch of hyssop in the blood of Christ and sprinkled it on the mob crowded about the cross, doing this in mockery of the Jewish rite of purification mentioned above. In the absence of any other explanation, this conjecture seems plausible.

e) A representation of pincers holding a single nail, or of pincers and three nails, is frequently used to symbolize the lowering of Christ's body from the cross.

Practically every detail of the records in the Gospels, which tell the story of Christ's passion, death and resurrection, has been represented in Christian art by a symbol. We have recorded and described the most important symbols, those most likely to be seen in stained glass church windows, in carvings, and other places.

II. THE CROSS

Before a sinful, war-smitten world, in which "man's inhumanity to man makes countless thousands mourn,"

[7] Mark 14:68, 72.

[8] Numbers 19:6, 18; Psalm 51:7. *See also* article "Hyssop," Hasting's *Dictionary of the Bible.*

the Cross of Christ stands as an everlasting sign of God's suffering love and plan of redemption. Among all the symbols that Christians cherish, none is so precious as the cross. It is no cause for wonder, then, that this symbol has been more variously presented than any other and has never lost its potency to melt the hearts of men.

Dr. W. L. Stidger tells movingly the following story of an experience he had one night in France during World War I:

The first time I drove my truck down the Toul road I was frankly scared. Not of the shellfire which peppered that important road all night long. No, my fear was that somewhere I would take the wrong turning with my load of supplies for the men in the front line and drive straight into the German lines. I had a map, of course, but I was never a very good map reader.

It was winter and the road was full of shell holes, ice hummocks and boggy stretches of mire. After ten miles of cautious driving, without lights, I was sure that I had lost my way. Just then I came to a crossroad. I knew that one of the forks led straight into "No Man's Land" and thence into the German lines. The other would take me to my destination. But which was which?

I stopped the truck and saw, gleaming through the darkness, the shadow of a cross. I went over to it with my shaded flashlight. Perhaps, beneath the crucifix, there would be a sign. There was. It showed me the right road, which was not the one I was about to take! I uncovered my head and flashed my light up over the crucifix itself, which bore a beautiful carved body of Christ—a little masterpiece of reverential artistry. Then my flashlight fell on the sentence above it. The words, in French, were: "Traveler, hast thou ever seen so great a grief as Mine?"

Never did a single sentence carve itself so deeply and vividly on my mind as that one. Off in the distance I could hear the roar of the big guns. But there was a new peace and confidence in my heart as I climbed back into my truck and delivered my load of supplies.

To this day, whenever I think of the loneliness, suffering and heartbreak of war, I remember that night on the Toul road and the sentence carved above that French crucifix.[1]

A reliable authority states that there are more than four hundred forms of the cross, of which about ten per cent are generally used in Christian art, the remainder being mostly of interest to students of heraldry, architects and artists.[2]

The scope of this book permits representation of only a few of the crosses which we are apt to see in churches. However, at least two crosses are included, advisedly, which ought to be avoided in Protestant churches, because use of them would be quite improper. They appear as Figure 14 and Figure 15 in Plate G.

Figure G1 is known as the Tau cross because it resembles the Greek letter of that name. Tradition says that the "pole" with a brazen serpent, lifted up by Moses in the wilderness, was of this shape.[3] The rise and persistence of this tradition may have been caused by the allusion in John 3:14. Tradition also says that a Tau cross was the sign made by the Israelites on the doorposts of their houses, in Egypt, on Passover night.[4] The Tau cross is generally regarded as a primitive pre-Christian

[1] "Getting the Most Out of Life," *Chicago Daily News*, October 1, 1941. Used by permission.

[2] F. R. Webber, *Church Symbolism*, Jansen, Cleveland, 1938 (contains nearly a hundred illustrations of various crosses).

[3] Bishop Wm. Durandus (thirteenth century), in his *Rationale Divinorum Officiorum*, suggests that anciently the Tau cross was used as a charm to drive away evil things and spirits, in this case, the evil being symbolized by the serpent. *See also* Num. 21:9.

[4] Exod. 12:22.

THE CROSS
(PLATE G)

cross, associated by Christian tradition with the Mosaic dispensation.

Anciently, the use of the Tau cross as a symbol of the generative principle in Nature was common. During their bondage in Egypt, the Hebrews became familiar with the key-like Egyptian ankh, a symbol of life and immortality. (See accompanying illustration.) In Christian usage this symbol refers to immortality.[5]

Figure G2 is the ancient Anchor Cross of the catacombs. Obviously it combines an anchor and a cross, thus symbolizing both hope in the life eternal and salvation from sin through the merits of the Savior's death and resurrection. The origin of this form of cross is probably related to Hebrews 6:19. This cross is sometimes called *Crux Dissimulata* because, like the fish symbol described in chapter 4, its use was intended to conceal its true significance from spies and informers, intent on persecution. The similarity of the cross bar of an anchor to that of a cross made the disguise effective. When seen in a church window, this symbol ought to teach us reverence for the early saints, whose persistence of faith under persecution insured transmission to us of the privileges of the Christian gospel.

Figure G3 is the Latin Cross—the form of cross on

ANKH

[5] Frequently referred to as *Crux Ansata,* literally "the cross with the handle." Sir Ernest Wallis Budge, in his work on *Amulets,* says that Rawlinson was mistaken in assuming the ankh to be a form of cross. It was used ! y the Egyptians as a symbol of the life force and as such was also used to signify immortality. Use of the ankh as a Christian symbol is comparatively rare. *See* Elizabeth Goldsmith, *Ancient Pagan Symbols,* Putnam's, 1929, p. 42.

which Christ was crucified. Therefore, it is the pre-eminent symbol of Christianity. Figure G4, the Graded Cross, is a Latin cross on a base of three steps from which it derives its name. They represent, in descending order, Faith, Hope and Charity (in Latin, *Fides, Spes, Caritas*).

Figure G5 is called Saint Andrew's Cross, because it is believed that Saint Andrew, at his own request, was crucified on this form of cross, counting himself not worthy to die on the same kind of cross as his Lord. It is said that, while dying slowly on it, he continued to preach to those around him. It is the emblem of the Brotherhood of Saint Andrew, as well as the national cross of Scotland. In liturgical churches, this cross is used to indicate the beginning of the Church Year, which is determined by the Sunday nearest Saint Andrew's Day. This cross is sometimes called Saint Patrick's Cross. It is a particularly significant emblem for use in any church called Saint Andrew's.

Figure G6, the Greek Cross, also called the Cross of Saint George, is of ancient use and probably had its origin among the esthetically-minded Greeks who had an eye for perfect symmetry in all artistic matters. Its arms are of equal length, which facilitates use of it for decorative purposes.

Figure G7 is commonly known as the Celtic or Irish Cross, and is sometimes called the Cross of Iona, because an ancient example is found on the Isle of Iona in western Scotland. Iona is the point at which the Irish missionaries first established a foothold in Scotland. Without doubt, it is one of the most interesting variant forms of the Latin cross having ecclesiastical origin. Several notable examples of it are well preserved in Ireland. Some of them have been visited and examined by the author. The carvings are usually quite elaborate, as

THE CROSS OF MONASTERBOICE

in the case of the Cross of Monasterboice, near Drogheda, which is pictured above.[6]

---

[6] J. R. Allen, in his book, *Early Christian Symbolism in Great Britain and Ireland*, London, 1887, p. 136, on the basis of information contained in *The Annals of the Four Masters*, conjectures that this famous cross was made by Muiredeach, *circa* A.D. 923. The principal subject on such crosses is usually the crucifixion.

Apparently this type of cross was commonly erected in cemeteries in ancient times in Great Britain and Ireland, and it may be seen frequently in American cemeteries today. The circle is emblematic of eternity. Probably, the original intention in using the circle was to signify the eternal effect of the redemption secured on the cross by the death of Christ. The vertical member of this cross tapers and the slightly bulging effect known as entasis is sometimes employed in designing the upright part.

Figure G8 is known as the Maltese Cross. It is also called the Regeneration Cross, because it symbolizes the new birth. It appears to be composed of four spearheads which meet at a central point. The eight outer points symbolize the eight Beatitudes. This cross derives its common name from the Island of Malta, because it was the emblem of the famous Knights of Saint John, or Knights Hospitallers, organized some time in the eleventh century to protect Christian pilgrims on their way to Palestine to visit the Holy Sepulcher. The Order was banished from the Island of Rhodes by the Turks and thereafter was permitted by Charles V to settle on the Island of Malta. The Maltese Cross is the symbol of Saint John's Day. Saint John the Baptist was the patron saint of the celebrated Knights aforementioned. The Maltese Cross should be carefully distinguished from the Cross Patée (meaning broad-footed), shown in Figure G10, the arms of which curve gracefully, whereas, the arms of the Maltese Cross are composed of straight lines.

Figure G9 is known as the Jerusalem Cross, sometimes

71

called the Crusader's Cross. It was on the coat of arms of the Latin Kingdom of Jerusalem (A.D. 1099–1203) as well as on the coat of arms of the famous Godfrey of Bouillon, its first ruler. It was designed after the pattern of a cross which Godfrey found somewhere in Asia Minor. This cross is composed of four Tau-shaped crosses with their bases conjoined at the center. The four adjacent semi-enclosed Greek crosses are said to represent the Four Gospels which have displaced the Mosaic Law represented by the Tau crosses. Other interpreters say that the large cross represents the sword-wound in the Savior's side, and the four small crosses the prints of the nails in his hands and feet.

The Jerusalem Cross has also been interpreted as signifying Christian missions, the large cross standing for the early Christian Church at Jerusalem and the four small Greek crosses signifying the four corners of the earth. Because the Tau-shaped arms of the large cross resemble ancient crutches, this cross is said to symbolize Christ's power to heal bodily and spiritual ills. This symbol is amazingly rich in historic significance and Christian teaching.

Figure G11 shows the Cross Patée Fitched, the latter word meaning pointed. Remove the points and there remains the Cross Patée. Figure G11 is a very decorative form of this cross which is sometimes used on altar cloths and other church furnishings.

The Cross Fleurie (French: "flowery"), Figure G12, is another very beautiful cross frequently seen embroidered on altar cloths. On each arm there are three petals, which suggest the effect of a flower, hence the name. A somewhat similar cross is the Cross Patonce (a name derived from the paw of the ounce or panther) in which the arms are more expanded.

Figure G13 is known as the Budded Cross, the arms of which terminate in trefoil form, thus symbolizing the Holy Trinity. This form of treatment can be applied also to the Greek Cross.

Figure G14 is the Papal Cross. It has three transverse arms, each a little longer than the other, in descending order. It is borne before the Pope, in procession, as the emblem of his high office. Therefore, it cannot properly be used in the decorations of Protestant Churches. The two upper cross bars are said to signify the crosses of the malefactors who were crucified beside our Lord on Calvary. A cross having a long transverse bar, with a short transverse bar a little distance above it, is known as the Patriarchal Cross. In early paintings patriarchs are shown carrying it, hence the name. Later it became associated with distinguished members of the Roman Catholic hierarchy, such as archbishops and cardinals. It differs from the Papal Cross in having only two cross arms instead of three.

Figure G15 shows the Russian Cross, also known as the Slavic Cross and as the Eastern Cross. The upper bar represents the tri-lingual superscription placed on the Cross of Christ by order of Pontius Pilate. The slanting bar has been interpreted in several ways, but it seems the most correct interpretation is that this so-called "foot-rest" really represents one member of a Saint Andrew's Cross, the other arm lying along the main upright beam. According to tradition, Saint Andrew was the first Christian missionary to Russia. The Slavic cross is used on the spires of Eastern Orthodox Churches. For this reason, and in order to avoid confusion, it should not be used on Protestant churches.

The cross illustrated in Figure G16 is often called the Cross of Triumph, or the Cross Triumphant. It consists of a Latin Cross erected on a banded globe, denoting the triumph of the Christian Gospel over the world. Sometimes, in religious paintings, one sees Christ, or the Christ-child holding in his hand a cross and orb of somewhat similar design. Figure G16 is a favorite emblem for stained glass windows and is appropriate for artistic use in subjects dealing with Christian missions.

The swastika is an ancient symbol of unknown origin, consisting of a cross with equal arms which are bent at right angles. Apparently, in pre-Christian times it was connected with sun-worship and the origin of fire. The early Aryan peoples named the two arms *pramatha* and *swastika* and both of them combined were called *arani*. When this symbol was reproduced in wood and one arm was revolved quickly against the other, fire or *agni* was produced. In all probability, there is a direct connection between *pramatha* and the Greek fable of Prometheus. The swastika was used in the catacombs, by the early Christians, doubtless with reference to Christ as "the Sun of Righteousness." The word swastika is of Sanscrit origin—*su*, good; *asti*, being; and the suffix *ka*, the whole being equivalent to "It is well" and implying resignation to things as they are. It is symbolic of life, movement, pleasure. It was reverenced in India, China and other Oriental countries for at least three milleniums before the coming of Christianity. Dr. Hein-

SWASTIKA   TRISKELION

rich Schliemann ex-
humed objects on the
site of ancient Troy
which were marked with
this symbol. It is very
widely distributed, and
occurs in Mayan sym-
bolism as well as in the
symbolism of the old
world cultures. It is
sometimes called the
fylfot (many-footed)
cross, a designation of
Anglo-Saxon origin.

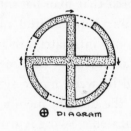

DIAGRAM

The triskelion (Greek for three legs) is a symbol of the sun intended to express motion. A similar device, with four legs, called a tetraskelion, is a modifi-cation of the swastika. In the accompanying illustra-tion, below the swastika and the triskelion, a diagram of a circle enclosing a cross is shown, with pieces of the circle cut out to indicate movement. This diagram offers an explanation of the probable origin of the swastika and of the closely related triskelion and tetraskelion. If one looks at the sun, or any bright light, with eyelids almost closed, a cross of light appears, the transverse beam being probably caused by the reflection of light along the edges of the eyelids. Thus primitive man came to associate the circular shape of the sun with a cross originating within the circle.

To primitive peoples the life force and the sun as the nourisher of life were of enormous importance. They worshiped what they esteemed most highly. That is what every man does. He bows down to that which he regards as having the greatest *worthship,* whether it be God, power, money or something else.

Before closing this chapter, the curious fact should be noted that man has introduced the cross symbol into the four fundamental mathematical operations which are most intimately related to his economic life and mental culture. A cross with arms of equal length placed between figure-symbols denotes addition. Take away the upright member of the cross and subtraction is indicated. Swing it around from the plus position and make the ends of two arms of the cross rest on the line and you have the sign of multiplication, which is an acceleration of addition. Represent one member of the cross as complete and the other as diminished to two points, and fragmentation or division is indicated.

Whether he enters a Christian church or not, a man, in his everyday life, cannot escape this ubiquitous symbol of something that lies deep beneath the surface of human nature and that seems to inhere in the life process itself.

CHAPTER VI

Symbols on "The Great Chalice of Antioch"

IN THE YEAR 1910, some Arab workmen, digging in the ruins of ancient Antioch in Syria, found a mass of silver which consisted of a cross, three book covers, and two chalices—one small, the other large. For the sake of distinction, the large chalice has been called "the Great Chalice of Antioch."

This remarkable find has aroused great interest throughout Christendom. It is believed that these articles were hidden by the sacristan of the Cathedral of Antioch during the persecution of the Christians in that city, under Julian the Apostate, in A.D. 362, or when the cathedral was destroyed by Chosroes II, of Persia, in A.D. 611.

Distinguished experts, including the noted authority on Christian antiquities, Professor Josef Stryzgowski of Vienna, have come to the conclusion that the date of the large chalice should be placed about the end of the first century. Its form is similar in style to that of cups found in an excavated villa, near Mount Vesuvius, which was covered with lava when Vesuvius erupted in A.D. 79.

The crude silver inner cup set in the elaborately decorated container (see illustration on page 79) was undoubtedly much venerated in the early Church and apparently pieces were anciently cut from the rim of it to be used as relics. This mutilation is plainly evident in the picture.

It has been surmised that the inner cup might have been used at the institution of Holy Communion by our Lord. Of course, that cannot be proved, but there must have been some very important reason for preserving this rude inner vessel. Its capacity is estimated, by Dr. George A. Barton, at nearly three quarts of liquid, enough for the Paschal meal of a small group. Fortunately for posterity, the container was overlaid with gold leaf, which acted as a preservative and made it possible for modern Christians to view, in good condition, the most remarkable relic of the early Church.

It is the property of Mr. Fahim Kouchakji, through whose kindness the author was able to obtain an excellent photograph of it. For the purpose of this book, our interest centers chiefly in the symbolism on the container.

Above the beaded border, at the base of the bowl, twelve grape vines reach upward and form twelve loops, in each of which there is depicted a seated figure, surrounded by branches, leaves, tendrils and grape clusters. The central figure is that of Christ (see illustration). He is also represented in more youthful form as the central figure on the reverse side (not seen in the picture). The ten seated figures on the chalice have distinctive features and are believed to represent Peter, Paul, James the Less, Jude, Andrew, Luke, Mark, Matthew, John, and James the Greater.

Photo by courtesy of Mr. Fahim Kouchakji, New York

THE GREAT CHALICE OF ANTIOCH

Examination of the details appearing in the picture reveals birds, symbolic of the faithful, resting upon the branches of the vines, near clusters of grapes which symbolize the Blood of Christ. The seated figures are shown pointing to Christ the central figure, as if bearing testimony and giving adoration. Beside Christ, there is a lamb signifying his sacrificial death. The right hand of Christ is represented as touching a plate on which are five loaves and two fishes, placed beside a dove. Supposedly, this central group is symbolical of Jesus Christ, as the Lamb of God, on whom the Holy Spirit descended in the form of a dove, giving food to the world. Under the feet of Christ is an eagle, perhaps symbolic of the Roman empire, destined in due time to acknowledge his overlordship. Below the Roman eagle is a basket placed between two bunches of grapes. The last mentioned group may refer to the passages in Saint John's gospel, in which is contained the characteristic sacramental teaching illustrated on the chalice.[1] For a constructively critical study of the chalice, see Dr. George A. Barton's *Archeology and the Bible*, published by the American Sunday School Union, Philadelphia, 1933, pages 559–563.

[1] John 6:51–58; 15:1–5.

CHAPTER VII

Symbolic Stars

STARS FIGURE PROMINENTLY in the symbolic language of the Holy Scriptures, both in the Old and New Testaments, particularly with reference to the promise of the Messiah and regarding Jesus Christ.[1]

Figure H1, the five-pointed star with rays emanating from it, is known variously as "the Star of Jacob," "the Star of Jesse," "the Star of Bethlehem" and "the Star of Epiphany," meaning "manifestation or showing," from the Greek *epi*, "upon," and *phanein*, "showing."

Contrary to common belief, this star is not an authentic Christmas symbol. Its Christian use is properly related to the Epiphany; *i.e.*, to the showing or manifestation of the child Jesus to the Gentiles, represented by the "wise men from the East," who sought the royal infant of David's line, because they had observed the star but did not know the exact place of birth. They went first to Jerusalem seeking guidance to the birthplace of the expected Jewish Messiah. Then, acting on the information obtained, they went to Bethlehem and, according to Saint Matthew, saw the Holy Child in a "house." Apparently Jesus had been removed from the stable before the time of their appearance—a fact which invalidates the traditional artistic treatment of

[1] Num. 24:17; Isa. 60:3; Matt. 2:1, 2; II Pet. 1:19; Rev. 22:16.

SYMBOLIC STARS
(PLATE H)

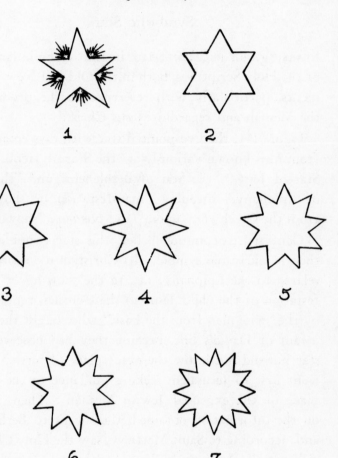

the scene.[2] (When it suits their fancy, artists and poets are apt to treat such matters with license.) Another example is that in which the Scripture record states that Mary wrapped the new-born babe in "swaddling clothes," [3] but nearly all the pictures present him as naked.

The five-pointed star is sometimes grouped with symbols of the Virgin Mary. In a way, this is peculiarly appropriate, because the Hebrew word for Mary is Miriam, which means a star.

Figure H2, the six-pointed star, has been discussed already in a previous chapter as a compound Trinitarian symbol, also as "the Star of David," (see page 49). It is also called "the Star of Creation," this name having reference to the last sentence of Genesis 1:31. It is sometimes employed as an emblem of God the Father, the six points referring to his attributes: power, wisdom, majesty, love, mercy and justice. The use of this star as a symbol probably antedates the beginnings of recorded history.

Figure H3, the seven-pointed star, known as "the Mystic Star," is an emblem of "the seven gifts of the Holy Spirit." Sometimes the initials of the Latin words for the gifts as stated in Revelation 5:12 are written on the points.[4]

Figure H4, the eight-pointed star, is the "Star of

[2] F. R. Webber, *Church Symbolism*, Jansen, Cleveland, 1938, p. 60.
[3] A universal custom in Palestine. *See* James Neil, *Everyday Life in the Holy Land*, Cassel, London, 1913, p. 59.
[4] The usual Latin rendering of this list is: *Virtus, Divinitas, Sapientia, Fortitudo, Honor, Gloria, Benedictio.*

83

Baptism," or "Star of Regeneration," because the number eight is symbolic of rebirth. Baptismal fonts are usually octagonal in shape, the eight sides having reference to the idea of regeneration in baptism, a doctrine held by Catholics. The origin of this symbolic usage is lost in the mists of antiquity. It is supposed by some that it goes back to the story of the Flood,[5] according

to which eight souls were saved in Noah's Ark. Bishop Durandus (thirteenth century) avers that, as seven days were occupied by God in creation and rest, the eighth day was significant of "the new creation" or regeneration—a divine octave.

Some of the earliest fonts were either round- or square-shaped. The octagonal form, while used early, was not in common use until the thirteenth

THE CLONARD FONT

century. The accompanying picture illustrates ancient practice in the construction of octagonal fonts. The font pictured here was made by skilled Irish craftsmen for use in the monastery founded by Saint Finien at Clonard, Ireland, about A.D. 527. According to the late Dr. P. W. Joyce, it is still in existence and fairly well preserved.

Figure H5, the nine-pointed star, is a symbolic repre-

[5] Gen. 1:13; 7:18.

84

sentation of the nine Fruits of the Holy Spirit.[6]   Sometimes the nine Fruits are represented by the initials of the Latin words used in rendering the passage in the fifth chapter of Galatians.   The list in Latin is as follows: *Caritas, Gaudium, Pax, Longanimitas, Benignitas, Bonitus, Fides, Mansuetudo, Continentia.*

Figure H6, the ten-pointed star, refers to the ten disciples who (counting out Judas and Simon Peter) neither betrayed nor denied Jesus.

Figure H7, the twelve-pointed star, may be employed to symbolize either the twelve tribes of Israel or the twelve apostles chosen by our Lord.   The large silver star which was placed in the floor of the Grotto of the Church of the Holy Nativity, in Bethlehem, in the nineteenth century, at the supposed spot on which Jesus was born, has twelve points.[7]   Tradition associates the number twelve with closeness of relationship between the divine and the human.

Formerly, the Feast of Epiphany was known as "Twelfthtide," or "Twelfth Day," because it falls on the twelfth day after Christmas.

[6] Gal. 5:22, 23.

[7] It was a row over the placement of this star that provoked the Crimean War.

CHAPTER VIII

Symbols of Doctrines and Ideas

GROUPED IN PLATES I and J we have a number of interesting symbols, a good many of which are in common use. Others are given because they may be seen occasionally and it is well to know their significance.

The first figure in Plate I is the circle, which has neither beginning nor end. It is symbolic of the eternal existence of God.

In Figure I2 a globe encircled by a serpent is the symbol of the fall of man through temptation by a serpent—the devil (see Genesis, third chapter). The words in Latin, *Ipsa conteret caput tuum* (It shall bruise thy head), occur in Genesis 3:15.

Figure I3 shows the rose as the symbol of Messianic promise. The prophet Isaiah foretells that "the desert shall rejoice, and blossom as a rose." [1] The form of rose in this symbol is conventional and it is said that the use of it originated about the thirteenth century.

Figure I4 illustrates the censer as symbolic of worship, prayer, adoration.[2]

In Figure I5 we have the anchor as a Christian symbol of very early occurrence. It was used freely in the catacombs and is based on Hebrews 6:18, 19, "the

[1] Isa. 35:1.
[2] Lev. 16:12; Rev. 8:3.

hope set before us: which we have as an anchor of the soul." The anchor has been discussed in an earlier chapter as a form of disguised cross symbolizing hope in Jesus Christ. A familiar combination of emblems is a cross, an anchor and a heart, these signifying *faith, hope and love.*

The ox symbolizes strength, patience and sacrifice in Figure 16. Sometimes the ox is shown with an altar on the left and a plough on the right, signifying that he is ready for either sacrifice or work.[3] The use of the figure of an ox as a Christian symbol is probably based on the words of our Lord, recorded in Matthew 11:30, "For my yoke is easy, and my burden is light." A winged ox is the symbol of Saint Luke the Evangelist, because in his gospel there is a lengthy description of the sacrificial death of Christ.

In Figure 17 the origin of the shield as an emblem signifying trust is found in Ephesians 6:16, in which Saint Paul describes the armor of a Christian, including "the shield of faith." This passage of Scripture is richly symbolical.

Figure 18 is a pointed arch which signifies aspiration and striving for growth in the spiritual life. It is a characteristic feature of Gothic church architecture.

The burning torch in Figure 19 is a symbol of pagan origin. Renaissance artists used it as a symbol of the Nativity of our Lord. It also signifies the witnessing of

[3] The idea may have been derived from the festival of the Bouphonia, at Athens, in which an ox was sacrificed, his skin stuffed and the effigy then set up and yoked to a plow, thus symbolizing death and resurrection. *See* Jane Harrison, *Ancient Art and Ritual*, Henry Holt and Co., 1913, pp. 89–91.

Christians: "Even so let your light shine before men; that they may see your good works, and glorify your Father who is in heaven." [4]   It is not used in Christian art with reference to Christ as "the Light of the World," this purpose being served by two altar candles.

Figure I10 shows the cross and crown, as a symbol, referring to death and post-mortem reward. [5]   Since ancient times, the crown has been used to symbolize the reward of the faithful in the life that lies beyond the death of the body. [6]

Figure I11.   Here we have palm leaves, like the crown, to signify the victorious Christian's reward when this life is over. [7]   Anciently, palm leaves were often given, as a prize or mark of distinction, to the winners in contests of strength and skill.   The Latin saying, *"Palmam qui meruit ferat"* (let him bear the palm who merits it), originated from this custom.

In Figure I12, heads of wheat symbolize "the Bread of Life." [8]   This is a favorite symbol of Holy Communion and together with clusters of grapes (see Figure J12) is often found on communion tables and altars.

Figure J1 illustrates the lily.   In Christian art, the lily signifies the virginity of Mary, the Mother of our Lord.   It also signifies purity, innocence, heavenly bliss. The Madonna Lily (*Lilium candidum*) is the one most commonly employed in presenting this symbol, especial-

[4] Matt. 5:16.
[5] Rev. 2:10.
[6] Jas. 1:12; I Pet. 5:4.
[7] Rev. 7:9, 10.
[8] Mark 14:22.

SYMBOLS OF DOCTRINES AND IDEAS
(PLATE I)

1. CIRCLE   2. SERPENT   3. ROSE

4. CENSER   5. ANCHOR   6. OX

7. SHIELD   8. POINTED ARCH   9. TORCH

10. CROWN   11. PALM LEAVES   12. WHEAT

SYMBOLS OF DOCTRINES AND IDEAS
(PLATE J)

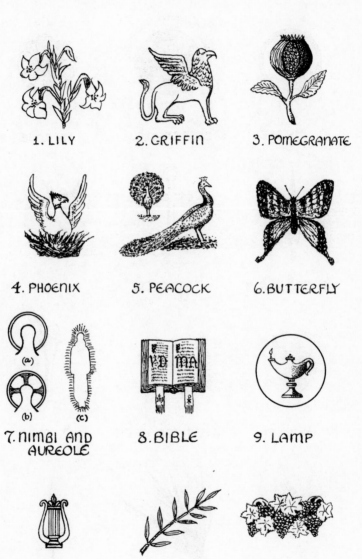

1. LILY   2. GRIFFIN   3. POMEGRANATE

4. PHOENIX   5. PEACOCK   6. BUTTERFLY

7. NIMBI AND   8. BIBLE   9. LAMP
AUREOLE

10. LYRE   11. OLIVE BRANCH   12. GRAPES

ly in connection with the Annunciation. The lily, as a symbol of Easter, refers to the fact that a bulb decaying in the soil produces a new bulb, stem, leaves and flowers, all rising in glory above the dark soil in which the process of death and the release of new life are inseparable, thus signifying the attainment of immortal life though the body perish. This is one of the most beautiful and significant symbols employed in Christian art.

Figure J2 shows the griffin, or gryphon (from the Greek *grupos,* meaning "hook-nosed"), as a fabulous animal, with the wings and beak of an eagle and the body and legs of a lion. In Christian art, it signifies the divine and human nature of our Lord, the eagle-like portion referring to his divinity and the lion-like portion to his humanity.

Figure J3. Here we have a bursting pomegranate, a symbol of the resurrection of our Lord and also of the resurrection of his faithful followers. It therefore symbolizes the hope of new life because it is split by the pressure of its many seeds, by which is signified fecundity or the power to reproduce life. It is a fitting emblem for use on an altar or paraments.

Figure J4. Like the griffin, the phoenix is fabulous. Apparently the word is derived from the Greek word *phoinix,* a date-palm tree. The ashes of burned date-palm trees were anciently regarded as the best fertilizer for their seedlings. Some think that this may explain the origin of the fable about a strange bird that came up from the ashes of the fire in which it had been burned and was therefore regarded as an emblem of resurrection.

91

Significantly, in Byzantine art, the date-palm tree and the phoenix are both employed as symbols of the resurrection.

Figure J5. In the early church, the peacock was a common symbol of resurrection. When the peacock molts, he grows new feathers, more brilliant than those which he lost. This beautiful symbol is often found in stained glass windows today.

Figure J6. There is no finer symbol of the resurrection than the butterfly. From the larval stage, significant of the mortal life of mankind, it becomes a chrysalis, to all appearance without life, then suddenly it bursts the cocoon in which it was sealed and comes forth to soar into the sky with a new body and beautiful wings. So the human body, after death, is committed to the earth, but the spirit which once dwelt within it emerges into life everlasting.

Figure J7a. In Christian art, a nimbus (Latin for "cloud"), or circle of light surrounding the head of a saint, is emblematic of sanctity, and when employed in connection with any of the Persons in the Godhead, it signifies divinity. In the latter case, rays are always used, as in Figure J7b. The three rays are supposed by some to represent the three Persons in the Godhead. Others argue that they were originally intended to represent three arms of a Greek cross, the fourth being hidden by the figure. The meaning is not settled. Nimbus is the preferable term for the circle of light surrounding the head of a saint. The word halo has a somewhat different significance. It is derived from a Greek word which means disk, and is properly applied when the head of the figure is shown with an opaque lighted disk behind it. By way of reminder, it should be noted that the plural of nimbus is nimbi. Nimbi were used in pagan art as symbolic of divine power, in order to distinguish the gods from human beings. There are many variations of the nimbus. For instance, a rectangular or square nimbus has been used sometimes to indicate a living person; whereas, the circular form is invariably applied to dead persons and symbols of divine beings.[9]

In Byzantine art, one may see the Greek letters Omicron, Omega, Nu placed within the rays of the tri-radiant nimbus, as an abbreviation of the expression, "I am that I am" (see Chapter III, also Figure A9). Sometimes, in Italian art, one finds the name of the saint inscribed in his nimbus.

The aureole is an elongated form of nimbus surrounding the entire body of our Lord, and in Catholic churches it may be seen around the Madonna and Child. The "vesica piscis" form with pointed ends has been discussed already in Chapter IV. An aureole is often elliptical in form, with rounded ends. An aureole may consist of rays or flames of glory emanating from the figure, as seen in Figure J7c. An aureole may also take the form of a circle or a quatrefoil, when the composition calls for wider space than the elliptical form affords. An excellent book on the subject of nimbi and aureoles is

[9] The square nimbus is a peculiarity of Italian art. *See* W. and G. A. Audsley, *Handbook of Christian Symbolism*, Day, London, 1865, p. 26.

Major A. de Bles' *How to Distinguish the Saints in Art*, Art Culture Publications, New York, 1925.

Figure J8 is a Bible signifying "the Word of God." In this case the initial letters V.D.M.A. belong to the Latin words, *Verbum Dei manet (in) aeternum*, meaning "the Word of God remains forever."

Figure J9 shows the lamp as another symbol of the Word of God. Its origin is probably in Psalm 119:105.

Figure J10. The lyre is a symbol of music and, in Christian art, it signifies sacred music.

In Figure J11, we have the olive branch to signify peace, concord, healing. A crown of olive leaves signifies victory. A gnarled olive tree is a symbol of the Garden of Gethsemane and the Passion of our Lord.

Figure J12. Here we have grapes to signify the sacrament of Holy Communion or the Eucharist. Twelve bunches of grapes signify the Twelve Apostles. (See discussion of the symbolism on "the Great Chalice of Antioch" in Chapter VI.)

A thistle is frequently used to symbolize the Fall of Man and the consequent entry of sin into the world. It is sometimes used in conjunction with a symbol of Redemption.

A modern innovation coming into favor, in spite of the protests of conservatives who love only that which is established, is use of the passionflower as a symbol of the passion of our Lord. The name of this remarkable flower has reference to the fact that it contains representations of most of the passion symbols: The central column represents the pillar used for the scourging; the ovary represents the hammer used to drive the nails into the cross; the three styles represent the nails; the five stamens represent the five wounds; the ten petals represent the ten apostles who fled, leaving only Judas Iscariot, who betrayed his Lord, and John who went to Calvary and witnessed the Savior's dying agony. This flower serves better as a Christian symbol than some of the far-fetched and fabulous inventions of ancient times.

CHAPTER IX

Symbols of New Testament Characters

SYMBOLIC REPRESENTATION OF the Twelve Apostles is coming increasingly into favor among the evangelical churches today. This is peculiarly appropriate, because evangelical doctrines have their roots almost entirely in the teachings of the New Testament and the Apostolic Church. The commonly accepted symbols of the apostles and the evangelists are of ancient origin.

Plate K shows a set of such symbols on shields, but there are a good many permissible variations. Selection will depend on the preferences of the architect and the building committee.[1]

In Figure K1, we have the shield of Saint Peter which has an inverted cross, signifying that, by his request, he was crucified head downward, not considering himself worthy to be crucified in the same position as his Lord. The crossed keys (saltier) refer to Peter's confession and the power to forgive sins vouchsafed to the Church.[2]

Figure K2 shows the shield of Saint James the Greater with three scallop shells, symbolic of pilgrimage and missionary journeying. A common alternate is a pilgrim's staff with a hook and a wallet hung upon it. Sometimes a sword and scallop shell are used, the sword

[1] F. R. Webber, *Church Symbolism*, Jansen, Cleveland, 1938. This book is copiously illustrated and is an indispensable book for architects and artists concerned with church building and decoration.

[2] Matt. 16:13–19.

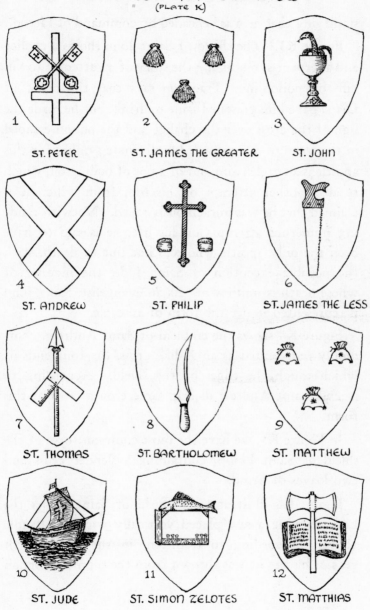

NEW TESTAMENT CHARACTERS
(PLATE K)

1. ST. PETER

2. ST. JAMES THE GREATER

3. ST. JOHN

4. ST. ANDREW

5. ST. PHILIP

6. ST. JAMES THE LESS

7. ST. THOMAS

8. ST. BARTHOLOMEW

9. ST. MATTHEW

10. ST. JUDE

11. ST. SIMON ZELOTES

12. ST. MATTHIAS

signifying that he was beheaded by command of Herod.[3]

Figure K3. The shield of Saint John shows a chalice and a serpent symbolizing the story of an attempt to kill him by poisoning. Tradition says that the priest of Diana gave him poisoned wine to drink, but he made the sign of the cross over the chalice and the poison escaped in the form of a serpent. An alternate symbol for this apostle is an eagle rising out of a pot of boiling oil, which recalls another attempt on his life, from which it is claimed that he was miraculously saved. Notwithstanding numerous attempts on his life, he is said to have been the only apostle who was not put to death, with the possible exception of Saint Jude, the manner of whose death is unknown. As an evangelist, Saint John is represented under the form of an eagle.

Figure K4 shows the emblem of Saint Andrew, commonly represented as an X-like cross, the four ends of which touch the edges of the shield. According to legend, Saint Andrew died in Greece on a cross of this form.

In Figure K5, we have the most common form of the shield of Saint Philip, containing a slender cross and two loaves of bread.[4]

Figure K6 illustrates the shield of Saint James the Less, showing a saw placed vertically with the handle above. According to tradition, in the ninety-sixth year of his age he was thrown from the topmost portion

[3] Acts 12:2.
[4] John 6:7.

of the Temple and his mangled dead body was sawn asunder.

Figure K7. The shield of Saint Thomas shows a vertical spear and a carpenter's square. Sometimes the square only is used. Tradition says that Saint Thomas went to East India as a missionary and erected a church with his own hands. He was shot with arrows and finally put to death by a spear in the hands of a pagan priest.

In Figure K8, we show the shield of Saint Bartholomew (believed by some to be the same as Nathanael) which contains a single flaying knife. Sometimes three knives are shown on the shield. Hippolytus is authority for the statement that Saint Bartholomew was seized by the Governor of Albanople, Armenia, and was flayed, crucified and beheaded. The author can never forget a picture portraying this cruel death which he saw in an old convent in Puebla, Mexico. One should be glad that Christian art today is sparing in its use of realism.

Figure K9. Here we have the shield of Saint Matthew as an apostle. It usually contains three purses which refer to his early occupation as a taxgatherer. As an evangelist, he is always portrayed as a winged man.

Figure K10 illustrates the shield of Saint Jude (known also as Thaddaeus or Lebbaeus), with a small sailing ship, symbolizing his missionary journeys. It is claimed that he went to Syria, and Arabia, and on into Mesopotamia, preaching the Gospel.

The shield of Saint Simon Zelotes, in Figure K11,

shows a fish lying on a book, the fish signifying that he was "a fisher of men," and the book signifying the Gospel. Frequently, he was the companion of Jude in missionary journeying.

In Figure K12, the shield of Saint Matthias, who was chosen by lot to succeed Judas Iscariot, shows an open Bible and a double-bladed battle-axe. It is said that he was beheaded because of preaching the Gospel, hence the meaning of the symbolism on the shield.

Frequently, one finds the shield of Saint Paul included with those mentioned above. His shield is shown in the center of Plate L. It contains an open Bible and a sword, symbolizing the Word of God as "the Sword of the Spirit" (*Gladius Spiritus*). There are several other symbols for this great apostle, but the one given is that most commonly used.

Purists in such matters say that the shields of the apostles should be displayed in the nave of the church, signifying the Church Militant, and not in the chancel, which signifies the Church Triumphant. This dictum is rather indifferently regarded, especially in evangelical churches. If a church is named after an apostle, it is most appropriate that his shield should be displayed at its main entrance, as is the case in the magnificent Protestant Episcopal Church of Saint Thomas in New York City.[5]

There is no standardized order in which the shields of the apostles should be shown. Geldart, in his *Manual*

[5] Visitors to New York City should not fail to see this impressive "sermon in stone," situated at Fifth Avenue and Fifty-third Street.

of Church Decoration and Symbolism, lists them as
follows: Saint Peter, Saint Andrew, Saint James the
Greater, Saint John, Saint Philip, Saint James the Less,
Saint Thomas, Saint Bartholomew, Saint Matthew, Saint
Simon Zelotes, Saint Jude, Saint Matthias.

The use of symbols for each of the Four Evangelists
is of early origin. Those most commonly used are four
winged creatures based on Ezekiel 10:14 and Revelation
4:7. The winged man is used to represent Saint Matthew because his gospel deals with the human genealogy
of our Lord [6] and throughout emphasizes his manhood.
The winged lion is used to represent Saint Mark, because of the allusion in Mark 1:3 to "The voice of one
crying in the wilderness," symbolized by a lion. In
Plate L, at the top of which appears the symbols of the
Four Evangelists, the famous "Lion of Saint Mark" is
represented. The lion is said to signify royalty, in allusion to the kingly office of Christ. The winged calf
is used to represent Saint Luke, whose gospel treats very
fully the atoning sacrifice of Christ, a calf or an ox
being the commonest symbol of sacrifice. The eagle,
believed to soar higher than any other bird, is the emblem of Saint John, because in his gospel he expresses
the divine nature of Christ in the most exalted terms to
be found in the New Testament. It is sometimes said
that these four figures signify, respectively, humanity,
royalty, sacrifice, divinity.

Occasionally, the symbols of the Four Evangelists are
placed on the four ends of a monumental cross, with

[6] Matt. 1:1–17.

NEW TESTAMENT CHARACTERS
(PLATE L)

 THE FOUR EVANGELISTS

1   2   3

THE MOTHER OF OUR LORD

  Spiritus Gladius

THE APOSTLE PAUL

ST. JOHN THE BAPTIST   ST. STEPHEN   ST. BARNABAS

the *Agnus Dei* at the center of the intersection. The use of these symbols in stained glass windows is very common. They are particularly useful where quatrefoil openings are employed in the plan of fenestration. In such openings they must be shaped in accordance with the space available. "The Lion of Saint Mark," shown at the top of Plate L, is not readily adaptable to this use. The preferred form would be that shown in the reredos cross illustrated on page 147.

In Plate L we have three shields, symbolic of the Virgin Mother of our Lord, which are appropriate for use in evangelical churches. The crescent moon refers to her glory, borrowed from Jesus Christ as "the Sun of Righteousness." In this symbol there may be a reference to the twelfth chapter of the Book of Revelation. The Fleur-de-Lys has been explained already as a conventionalized form of the Annunciation Lily; likewise, the rose as a symbol of the promised Messiah. The Mother of our Lord is the most distinguished woman in human history and, therefore, entitled to the profoundest respect.

At the foot of Plate L, three shields are shown. The one on the left signifies the coat of camel's hair worn by Saint John the Baptist, the one in the center refers to the death of Saint Stephen, whose martyrdom by stoning is described in Acts 7:57–60. His coat, represented on the shield, was laid at the feet of a young man named Saul, known after conversion as Paul. On the right is the shield of Saint Barnabas, who was stoned to death for the preaching of the Gospel. This is symbolized by the open Bible and three stones.

CHAPTER X

Symbolism of a Church

A NOBLE CHURCH STRUCTURE may be a "sermon in stone." However, a sermon of this kind is in a dialect which derives its peculiar terms, for the most part, from far distant times. This dialect is not difficult of mastery, and a working knowledge of it is bound to enhance the mood of reverence one naturally feels within a church built with sensitive regard for the best traditions in Christian art and architecture.

Most assuredly, one can worship God in a barn or a hall or any kind of structure, completely devoid of Christian symbolism or churchly character, but under such conditions the need for discipline of spirit is very great. God's presence is never wanting where two or three are gathered to worship him "in spirit and in truth." However, nowadays, there is general consent that, as an offset to the secular and paganizing influences which press upon us relentlessly in our daily lives, the church structure and its appointments should speak to us overtly of the higher life and of communion with that which is divinely uplifting and ennobling. Divine worship gives us our only breathing spell from the tensions set up by the modern way of life and nothing else can take its place. It is therefore more important than ever that the character of the church building should suggest a complete departure from the background against which we do our daily work. When we enter it, we should feel instinctively that we are standing on holy ground.

In an ideal church, the spire pointing upwards should be a reminder of things above, "where Christ sitteth at the right hand of God the Father." Its bell should proclaim the priority of worship over work and play. The open door of the church should say: "This is a house of prayer for all people." Its outside cross, whether rising above spire or gable, should remind us of the words of the Savior: "I, if I be lifted up, will draw all men unto me." Its altar and cross, as the center of the worshiper's visual interest, should call to mind the crucified and glorified Lord as well as the thought of the priesthood of all true believers, by virtue of which we can say, whether we be layfolk or ministers: "Then will I go unto the altar of God, unto God my exceeding joy. . . . ." [1] The candles upon the altar, when lighted during Holy Communion, should proclaim that Christ is "the Light of the World." The stained glass windows, filled with Christian emblems, should bring us messages from those far distant centuries in which Christians struggled through persecution, blood and tears to fight the good fight and finally win the crown of life. While reading in monograms and symbols the meaning of the secret signs which they devised in order that they might commune with one another in the fellowship of Christ, we feel a sense of oneness with them and there is impressed

[1] Ps. 43:4.

upon our minds, regardless of the flight of time, something of the deep meaning of "the communion of saints." In such ways, the Lord's house, when thoughtfully built and reverently used, can contribute greatly to the deepening of the life of the spirit.

In the past, many Protestant churches in America have been built with slight regard for the worship functions which a church proper should fulfill. One can see at a glance that the governing idea in their construction was to provide an all-purpose "auditorium" that would serve on almost any occasion. This object is understandable because, in many cases, the congregations could not afford to construct buildings really adequate to meet their needs. Most of these all-purpose buildings make little or no contribution to worship. If the services of worship in them are uplifting, it is generally in spite of the uninspiring surroundings. Many of these buildings are positively depressing in their effect on a sensitive mind.

Of late, all over the country, there seems to be a growing cognizance of this drabness of effect. We are witnessing numerous attempts to remedy it by partial alteration of the church interior so as to provide a "sanctuary" with an altar in full view and organ pipes more or less out of sight that previously stood behind the pulpit like a regiment of grenadiers at "Attention."

Sometimes the job is well done and produces a transformation in both the place and the worship services. In other cases, it is sometimes so badly botched as to advertise loudly to all the world that "it doesn't belong."

SYMBOLIC CHURCH PLAN
(CRUCIFORM)
(PLATE M)

EAST

ALTAR

SANCTUARY

ORGAN

CHANCEL

VESTRY

P

NORTH   N. TRANSEPT   CROSSING   S. TRANSEPT   SOUTH

NAVE

F
S

NARTHEX

L- Lectern
P- Pulpit

F - Font
S - Screen

WEST

Whether a congregation is building a new church, or altering an old one, the plans should be drawn and the work supervised by a competent architect. In either case, the governing considerations should be simplicity, comeliness and strength. Alteration is often the more difficult process, mainly because of obstacles in the existing structure, but sometimes because of obstacles in the minds of persons serving on the building committee.

A good many of the most impressive church buildings one sees are of cruciform plan, which embodies in the basic structure of the church Christianity's most important symbol. As this book is only very slightly concerned with church architecture, it is not within our purview to interpret anything except the outstanding general features of a cruciform church.

Referring to Plate M, we see the general effect of the ground plan, in the form of a cross. In looking at this cruciform plan, we first observe its relation to the points of the compass, the principal entrance being always at the west, and the sanctuary with the altar in the east. The wings of the transept correspond to the transverse bar on a Latin cross, they being named, respectively, north transept on the left, as one faces the altar, and south transept on the right. Of course, it is not always possible to build a church with "orientation" in this fashion. So, irrespective of the actual position of the building, the terms of direction are employed as indicated, and the east is known as the "ecclesiastical east," it being always at the head of the cross on the ground plan to which reference has been made already.

The custom of building churches on an east and west line may have had its origin in the ancient practice of facing Jerusalem when engaged in prayer. Perhaps, also, the rising of the sun in the east had something to do with it. If so, then the symbolism of "orientation" probably refers to the rising of "the Sun of Righteousness."

Beginning at the ecclesiastical west, we find a vestibule, sometimes called a narthex by pastors and architects. The historic reference of this term is not commonly understood. It is of Greek origin and means "rod." The Greeks used it as a name for the giant fennel, a rod-like plant. In the ancient Christian churches, constructed after Christianity emerged from hiding, it was customary to have an outside court, where unbaptized catechumens (Jews, converted heathen and others preparing for admission to membership) were permitted to stand and hear the first portion of the service of Holy Communion which corresponded in outline to the instruction and worship in the Jewish synagogues.[2] As the catechumens stood in the outer court, they looked through the openings between the columns (rods) which separated them from the congregation. Hence, the use of the term "narthex" for an outer court.[3]

Apropos of this interesting meaning of the term "narthex," it is significant that the early Christian services were conducted somewhat in the fashion of the pro-

[2] The Rev. Gerald Ellard, S.J., *Christian Life and Worship,* Bruce, Milwaukee, 1940, pp. 153 ff., shows how the "Liturgy of the Catechumens" corresponded with ritual procedure in the Jewish synagogues of that time, and is still retained in the Roman Missal without much change.

[3] *See* article "Narthex" in the *Columbia Encyclopedia.*

ceedings of a secret society, this perhaps, being the reason for the exclusion of the catechumens from witnessing the Holy Communion proper. Reference has been made already to the creed as esoteric. It was not permitted to be communicated in writing—only orally.

Gradually the times and the manners changed, and the significance of the narthex as an anteroom, occupiable under restrictions, disappeared. Today the term remains, but it has lost its historic meaning and is now a technical name for the vestibule in the west end of the church.

The main body of the church proper, lying between the west end and the chancel, is called the nave. This is a very interesting term, derived from the Latin word *navis,* meaning a ship. In the early days, the church, symbolically speaking, was the ark or ship of the Lord— the ship in which Christians sailed the sea of life.

In Plate M, the appropriate symbol is placed in a circle at the west end, as a reminder of the origin of the word "nave." The original temples of the Phoenicians were ships turned upside down. In the *Apostolic Constitutions,* a document that is said to date from the third century, directions are given for the building of a church: *"Sit aedes oblonga, ad orientum versus, navi similis"* (Let the building be oblong, toward the east, like a ship).

The layout in Plate M is quite general in character and only intended as a sketch of the most important particulars of the plan of a cruciform church. Going from west to east, there ought to be an unobstructed approach along the central aisle to the altar. This approach is emblematic of the Christian way to God. If the symbolic purpose were rigidly carried out, the baptismal font would be located, as in early times, near the

Hedrich-Blessing, photo   Courtesy of E. F. Jansson and R. Stoetze
NAVE AND CHANCEL, TRINITY METHODIST CHURCH, BEVERLY
HILLS, CHICAGO, ILLINOIS

beginning of this way, thus signifying ritual purification at the start of the journey. However, the baptismal font is now commonly placed near the front of the church so that the congregation may more readily see the ceremony of Baptism when performed.

Observe the word "crossing" in the plan. Sometimes

111

in liturgical churches, a removable "prie-dieu" (prayer desk) is placed in the center of the crossing for use of the minister, on certain occasions, when he joins the congregation and faces the altar to recite the litany in alternation with his people. After such use it is always removed so that there may be no barrier between the outer door and the altar.

In liturgical churches, it is customary to divide the eastern member of the cruciform plan into two sections: (1) the chancel, which is usually separated from the nave by a parapet or rail—the chancel floor usually being the height of three steps above the floor of the nave; (2) the sanctuary, which is generally elevated the height of three steps above the chancel and separated from it by a railing.

The height of the chancel should be governed by the length of the nave; the longer the church, the more steps at the chancel. The sanctuary contains the altar, which is raised at least one step above the level of the floor on which it stands. In many cases, it is raised three steps. When there are seven steps, in all, they are said to symbolize "the seven gifts of the Holy Spirit." But if there are three steps at the altar, they are said to symbolize the need for faith, hope and love in partaking of Holy Communion. Three steps may also be interpreted as symbolizing the Holy Trinity. The number and arrangement of steps will vary with the symbolic meaning intended to be expressed. Too many steps or steps too high are dangerous. The number and the height is largely an architectural problem.

At the front of the chancel is found the pulpit and lectern, the former for preaching and the latter for reading. In actual practice, one finds that the arrangement of the pulpit and lectern, as indicated in Plate M, may be reversed. There is no fixed rule governing this point, which apparently needs to be determined according to the location of the vestry, the lighting and other architectural considerations.

The English words, "cancel," "chancellor" and "chancel," come from a common source: the Latin word *cancelli,* which means lattice-screens. We cancel figures by drawing lattice-like lines across them. Originally, in ecclesiastical and civil courts, a chancellor was a law officer who sat behind a screen, a prototype of the modern bar in courts of law. The *cancellus,* or screen, in a church marks off the space called the chancel for occupation by those serving in a ministerial or liturgical capacity. In the chancel, the choir is seated on both sides of the approach to the altar, an arrangement suitable for antiphonal singing.

In liturgical churches, as the minister faces to the "east," the right side of the altar is called the "epistle-side" and the left side is called the "gospel-side," because the epistle and the gospel for the day are read in these positions respectively. In ancient times, the "north" was regarded as the place of heathen darkness to which the gospel was addressed symbolically by turning to the left side of the altar. It may not be a matter of moment, but if it is desired to fix these locations in mind, the key is found in the last two letters of the word "gospel"

113

which, when taken in reverse order, are the first letters of the word "left," thus giving the location of the "gospel-side" and, by inference, the "epistle-side."

In English parish churches, a heavy cross beam, known as a "rood beam," is often found at the place of separation of the chancel from the nave. The word "rood" is an early English form of the word "rod," and in its ecclesiastical meaning refers to the wooden cross which the beam bears at its center. Sometimes the beam is represented by an ironwork rood screen which serves the same purpose.

The sanctuary is the *sanctum*, or holy place, where the altar stands in the "east." Doubtless, the idea of the sanctuary and altar is derived, for the most part, from the structure of the Jewish temple. It should be emphasized also that Christian worship derives much of its character from the services of worship of temple and synagogue, especially the latter. Upon the altar, in the temple at Jerusalem, animal sacrifices were offered perennially on the Day of Atonement.[4] By the altar, the people of Israel were reminded that ". . . . apart from shedding of blood there is no remission."[5]

As Christ's death was the one full, perfect and sufficient sacrifice for all subsequent time, a Christian altar is a perpetual reminder of the oblation of God's only-begotten Son and therefore, fittingly, a place where we, in gratitude, offer our "gifts" unto God: bread and wine to be sanctified for "remembrance" of the Savior's suf-

[4] Lev. 16:29.
[5] Heb. 9:22.

ferings and triumph; money to be consecrated to the building of the Kingdom which he ushered in; flowers in thanksgiving for the beauty of the world in which we live, and as memorial symbols of our departed loved ones, who have entered eternal life through Jesus Christ.

It would be quite in line with ancient Christian practice to place a communion table, instead of an altar, in the sanctuary. The New Testament mentions both.[6] If a table is preferred, it should, of course, be centrally located like an altar. Either an altar or a communion table is to be treated as a means of worship and *never as an object of worship.*

The early Christians in Rome celebrated Holy Communion frequently; and as it was sometimes celebrated secretly in the catacombs, it was not unusual to place "the elements" on or near a tomb, perhaps the tomb of some beloved martyr who had yielded up his life for the cause of Christ.[7] This probably accounts for the origin of the so-called "tomb-altar," which is now the commonly accepted type.

The top of the altar is usually called the *Mensa,* or table, no doubt with reference to the early use of a table for the administration of the Lord's Supper. In liturgical churches, it is customary to incise five Greek crosses on the "Mensa," one at each of the four corners, and one, somewhat smaller than these, at the center. These crosses are emblematic of the five wounds in the

[6] I Cor. 10:21; Heb. 13:10.

[7] Saint Augustine mentions the practice of holding eucharistic services in the catacombs, and states that such a service was held when his mother's body was entombed. *See* Walter Lowrie, *Monuments of the Early Church,* The Macmillan Co., 1901, pp. 43, 44.

body of the Savior. At the back of the altar, in many cases, a retable or raised bench is set, and upon its center the cross is placed.[8] Generally on the altar there are two candles in candlesticks, one on either side of the cross. These candles should be lighted during the admin-

A MARBLE MENSA OF THE FIFTH CENTURY

istration of the Lord's Supper. They signify the divine and the human nature of Christ; also, when lighted, they signify that he is "the Light of the World." The origin of this usage may be connected with the necessity of using candles at the secret celebrations of Holy Communion in the catacombs. Probably, at first, the candles had no other significance. Nevertheless, the symbolism connected with them is exalted and worthy of observance in all Christian churches, no matter how simple the form of worship.

Sometimes, during administration of the Lord's Supper in evangelical churches, one may see seven smaller

[8] A well-proportioned altar looks better without a retable. The use of retables is of comparatively recent origin.

116

lights on each side of the cross, placed on upward-slanting seven-branched candlesticks. In this case, the lights are intended to signify "the seven gifts of the Holy Spirit." It is commonly accepted that there should be two candles only on the altar. An elaborate display of candles on an altar is not fitting in an evangelical church, except, perhaps, on festival occasions.

At the back of the altar, and rising above it, there is usually some kind of reredos, which may be more or less elaborate according to the means of the congregation. In many churches, the reredos is the most elaborately decorated part of the entire structure and often it is very rich in symbols. One frequently sees a curtain used in place of a reredos. This is called a dossal or dorsal (meaning back-piece). It is intended to heighten the effect of the altar, and should be planned with great care.

The flag of our country should not be placed inside the sanctuary proper, because its symbolism is primarily secular, but it should be placed close to the chancel rail in order to signify that we conceive of our citizenship according to religious principles. This should be emphasized by display of the Christian flag on the opposite side of the approach to the chancel.

Because, until recent years, these matters pertaining to the chancel and sanctuary have received only a slight degree of attention in non-liturgical churches, in the present transitional stage, the chancel and sanctuary are generally merged in one section[9] and, as a whole, called

[9] See illustrations of usage in evangelical churches in this chapter.

117

the chancel. As a rule, this section is shorter than the corresponding space in the Gothic structures erected by the liturgical churches. There is nothing to criticize

Courtesy of E. F. Jansson, Architect

INTERIOR, BAPTIST CHURCH, YPSILANTI, MICHIGAN
This chancel has a reversible altar, on the front of which appear the words, "Love Never Faileth," and on the reverse, which is presented during Communion, "This Do in Remembrance of Me"

about the unified arrangement. After all, in evangelical churches, we do not attach sacerdotal significance to the acts of the minister during the administration of the Lord's Supper.

In the liturgical churches and in some non-liturgical churches, such as The Methodist Church, it is customary for the communicants to kneel at the chancel rail to receive the elements during Communion. In other non-liturgical churches, the communicants receive the elements sitting in the pews. It might be just as well if there were no visible barrier between the congregation and the chancel, but only a removable rail for the purpose of receiving the elements while communing. This arrangement would be significant of the typically evangelical idea that the priesthood of believers is universal and that there should be no sign of a separating bar between those who serve at the altar and the people. We profess to be "workers together" in all things, including worship.

The structure, adornment and care of the altar was a major concern of the Hebrews.[10] Because of its symbolic importance, surely a Christian altar should be well built, adorned worthily, and thoughtfully respected. An altar, or a communion table, with a cross upon it, and with unobstructed central approach to it, is a definite aid in promoting social worship—in drawing the thoughts of the congregation to a focus on the great fundamental fact of the Christian faith set forth in John 3:16. The symbolism of the cross is eloquent throughout the service, and its message is likely to go with the people as they depart from the church, whether the sermon has been notable or otherwise.[11]

[10] Exod. 35:25; 39.
[11] See remarks by Rollin H. Walker, "A Forgotten Truth," *The Modern Message of the Psalms,* Abingdon Press, 1938, p. 63.

Moreover, if on a weekday, in response to the usual invitation displayed at the door, "Come in, Rest and Pray," one goes into a church and finds that the central

Courtesy of Dr. E. M. Conover
NAVE AND CHANCEL, TRINITY METHODIST CHURCH, ALBANY, NEW YORK

object forward is a pulpit, supported by a regiment of organ pipes, the effect is scarcely worth the effort. There is no call into the realm of the spirit, and one seldom or never sees an individual at prayer in such a church. On the other hand, if one beholds an altar and cross, no matter how plain, immediately the mind is drawn into contemplation of God's greatest gift to men.[12] The pulpit in the center raises a question mark, or leaves the mind cold; the altar and cross beget reverential humility, and put one in a mood to pray.

A good many altars are built too small to serve well during the celebration of the Lord's Supper, or to avoid the appearance of being overcrowded when vases of flowers and filled collection plates are placed there in addition to the cross and candlesticks.

An altar may be constructed fittingly of either wood or stone. In Catholic churches the top or "mensa" is always made of stone. It is well to employ a competent woodcarver or stonecutter to incise the symbolic decorations to be placed upon the surfaces of an altar. Perhaps the fewer of these decorations, the better, provided only that they be effectively executed. An IHS monogram, or an embellished Greek cross, in the center of the front will usually suffice as the major decoration. Any additional carving at the corners, or elsewhere, should be restrained in style. Intricate patterns and cryptic designs, displayed freely on the front of an altar tend to be distracting to the eye.

In case the altar has been constructed of very plain material, it may be advisable to cover the front with a colored cloth usually called a frontal. A white linen

---

[12] On the psychological reason for restoring the cross to its historic position in the sanctuary, see Andrew Blackwood, The Fine Art of Public Worship, Cokesbury Press, 1939, p. 93.

cloth is generally used to cover the Mensa and to this there may be attached a colored cloth, which may be allowed to hang over the front from five to eight inches deep, depending on the height of the altar. It is sometimes called a superfrontal, but the correct name is frontlet. The IHS monogram is generally embroidered on the center of the frontlet. In evangelical churches, it is frequently unadorned and therefore in harmony with evangelical simplicity. Perhaps a well-built altar of good material should be without front covering, except during the administration of the Lord's Supper.

One is likely to find a graded Latin altar cross in Protestant churches which have an altar. If it is small, it should be set on a retable, in order to give sufficient elevation. In non-liturgical churches, this cross is usually plain or, at the most, it contains only the figure of the *Agnus Dei,* or the IHS monogram in a circle placed at the middle of the transverse bar.

In evangelical churches, one very rarely sees a crucifix on the altar because the emphasis is on symbolizing the risen and glorified Lord rather than picturing the suffering of Christ. Perhaps, a lively imagination can supply as much thought of suffering as is needed to remind one of the Savior's agony, when one partakes of Holy Communion. Our forebears made up plenteously for the lack of an altar or crucifix in the church by constantly singing vivid hymns, such as "There is a fountain filled with blood, drawn from Immanuel's veins," a hymn which is realistic enough to satisfy the most ardent Catholic meditating on the death of Christ.

In support of Protestant reticence regarding the use of a crucifix portraying the suffering body of Christ on an altar instead of a plain cross, it should be observed that there is no proof that the use of a crucifix antedated the fifth century. Until the eleventh century, any representation of Christ on the cross was purely symbolic, the figure being always clothed, and generally robed and crowned as High Priest and King. The realistic picture-type of crucifix is of relatively late date. The obvious answer to the reproach of the late G. K. Chesterton, a convert to Roman Catholicism, about Protestants using a piece of cross-shaped wood or metal on an altar instead of using a crucifix, is that we prefer the earlier symbolical usage to the later realism.

True to its Arian drift, Gothic Christian art persistently fastened attention on the biological Jesus. In the northern European cathedrals, the figure of Jesus is generally portrayed as emaciated and tortured; not as a transfigured being, but one ostensibly defeated. Byzantine art was governed by a sounder instinct, which it expressed by magnifying the post-Calvary Christ, revealed as the Divine Word (Logos), glorified in fulfillment.

Those who favor the crucifix rather than the empty cross can quote Martin Luther, who said: "When I hear Christ preached, there is found in my heart, whether I choose it or not, the image of a Man hanging on a cross. . . . . If now it be no sin, but rather good for me, to have an image of Christ in my heart, why should it be sin to have one in my eye?" "Let each man be fully as-

123

sured in his own mind." [13]   No hard and fast rule is necessary.   However, it is proper that the prevailing preference in evangelical churches should be stated.

If a cross has been carved on the reredos, immediately above the altar, there should be no cross standing on the altar, but only two candles.   The same rule applies to a carving in relief of "The Last Supper" or to any elaborate set of figures immediately above the altar (see illustration on page 125).[14]   In England, before the Reformation, altars were mostly without crosses.   In the Church of Ireland (Episcopal), Canon Law does not permit the use of a cross on an altar.

Candlesticks and vases should be of the same material and finish as the cross.   In addition to these, during the administration of the Lord's Supper, there may be placed upon the altar a metal stand for the Service Book containing the Ritual.   Its front edge should be parallel to the edge of the altar.

Also, upon the altar, during the administration of Holy Communion, there should be "a fair linen cloth," sufficiently long to cover the top and drop over the ends of the Mensa or table-top, close to the floor.   A white linen cloth cover for the elements should be provided and, if desired, some fitting emblem may be embroidered on it.   Of course, this cover will remain in place until the minister is ready to proceed with the consecration of the elements.

[13] Rom. 14:5.
[14] Percy Dearmer, *The Parson's Handbook*, Oxford University Press, 1942, p. 86.

124

Courtesy of Dr. E. M. Conover

INTERIOR, PRESBYTERIAN CHURCH, VIRGINIA BEACH, VIRGINIA

Courtesy of Rev. Edward H. Busekros

CHANCEL, FIRST ENGLISH EVANGELICAL CHURCH, CHICAGO,
ILLINOIS

("Last Supper" scene carved on Reredos by Alois Lang)

125

Two large candles, one on each side of the cross, should be kept burning during the administration of Holy Communion. When lighted, they proclaim that Christ is "the Light of the World." Why have them if they are not to be lighted at that time? [15] As a general rule, candles should not be longer than the candlesticks in which they are set and, in any case, the tops of the candles should be lower than the head of the cross. Candles towering above the cross are out of proportion and they inevitably spoil the total effect of an altar.

The very common use of individual communion cups today for administration of the wine raises a practical question regarding the method to be used by the minister in its consecration and distribution. An ingenious writer on the subject suggests that a sufficiently large chalice be used for consecration, and that it be shaped with a lip from which the liquid can be subsequently poured, either directly into the individual communion cups, or into vessels designed for the purpose of filling such cups. He also suggests that each communicant, in going to the altar rail, pick up a cup from a tray conveniently placed near by. After communing, it can be placed quietly in a suitable rack fastened at the back of the communion rail. The feasibility of such procedure will depend on the number to be served. Some time ago, the author assisted at a Communion Service in which more than eleven hundred persons communicated, and the method suggested would have been impracticable.

[15] The old English Episcopalian Puritans scorned unlighted candles and observed: "the candles on our altars, most nonsensically stand unlighted, to signify what? the darkness of our noddles!"

In that case, the wine was consecrated in individual cups—the usual method, nowadays, in most evangelical churches. It is a radical departure from the ancient practice which has been abandoned with regret by many.

It is interesting to note that the method known as "intinction" is practiced in the famous Second Church of Newton, West Newton, Massachusetts (Congregationalist), described in a brochure entitled, "Our Church," printed in 1926: [16]

The individual comes forward and kneels down and receives for himself the body and blood of the Lord. The method used is that of intinction. The minister dips the edge of each wafer in the wine. The communicant receives this in the hand and immediately raises it to the lips, as the minister says: "The body and blood of our Lord Jesus Christ which was given for thee, preserve thy body and soul unto everlasting life. Take this in remembrance that Christ died for thee, and be thankful." This way of celebration emphasizes the individual's part in the sacrament. Everyone has to rise, come up the chancel steps and receive individually among the kneeling row of communicants at the rail.

It should be noted that this method is used at early communion services when the number of communicants makes it practical. When Communion is held in connection with the regular Sunday service, the deacons distribute the "elements" to the communicants in the pews. The minister must devise the best method he can, in keeping with denominational tradition as well as local conditions and, above all, in keeping with the dignity and solemnity of this most significant service of divine worship.

[16] Used by permission of Dr. Boynton Merrill, pastor.

It is customary to take up an offering for some worthy and appealing cause during the service of Holy Communion. This feature should be magnified and made specially significant; otherwise, it should be omitted. During Communion, as one looks on the Cross and thinks of Christ's great sacrifice, the moment and the emotion are peculiarly fitting for the making of a sacrificial gift for the poor, for missions, or some other great Christian enterprise. A small table, with collection plate, should be placed near the altar rail so that each communicant, in passing it, and just before kneeling, can deposit and consecrate his gift for Christ's sake.

It is fitting to state here that empty collection plates should never be permitted to stand upon the altar. While empty, they should be kept on a low shelf or table, preferably placed on the right side of the altar, as one faces it. In some churches, when the collection has been taken, it is customary to place quietly the contents of all the collection plates in one extra large plate. This is then carried to the altar by the person in charge of the collectors at the head of the return procession. Having arrived and arranged themselves as desired, the leader steps forward slightly in front of the others. The minister then receives the offering from him, and turning round, facing the altar, utters the appropriate prayer of dedication.

It is becoming that the prayer at the dedication of the offering should be simple, comprehensive and in keeping with the symbolism of the altar. For example:

128

O God of love, in whom we live and move, and by whom each of us is known, we lay these gifts on thine altar, with due thanks. From thee has come all that we have and, by what we give back to thee, we are the more made rich. Bless, now, our gifts and, through their use in thy church, bring nigh the day when peace and love shall dwell in all the earth. In the Name of Christ, our Lord, we ask. Amen.

As an alternative, the following might be used for dedication of the offering at a Communion Service:

O God, who didst give thine only-begotten Son to die on the cross that by his death men might be saved from their sins, with humble hearts, we here offer unto thee a part of that which thou hast given to us, and ask that our thought for those in need, and this act for love's sake may be blest in fruit that will bring praise to the Name of Christ. Amen.

Whatever the method used, it should be conducive to the dignity which is surely requisite in all actions at the altar.

The writer saw recently a picture of an extensively remodeled chancel containing a beautiful altar and reredos, but, lo! upon the center of the altar there appeared, not a cross, but a vase full of flowers badly arranged and, on both sides of the vase, a heap of empty collection plates, not even neatly piled. Would one be surprised if a hat and overcoat were also found on the altar, where such a mistaken idea of its proper use prevails? With or without an altar, a Communion Service can be made interesting and profoundly significant, or dull and repelling, according to the minister's attitude and capability. Increasingly, the congregations in evangelical churches are asking that the Communion Service be treated as a vitally significant act of worship, worthy of thoughtful preparation on the part of both minister and people.

Courtesy of A. Frank Wickes

THE CHANCEL, UNIVERSITY PLACE CHRISTIAN CHURCH, CHAMPAIGN, ILLINOIS

A Baptist minister, who has quite successfully specialized in making the Communion Service in his church memorable and impressive, has recently published a series of brief addresses and plans for such services that will

130

reward one for the time which is given to its perusal.[17]

In the introductory chapter, he says something quite significant regarding the use of ritual:

When a part of the Christian church began to resent the formalism and ritual of the program of worship, it established in the place of these a free, simple and relatively unadorned order of service. This movement was more than a revolt of the Protestants against the Catholic form of worship. It was the expression of a normal type of mind and personality. The plea for simplicity was at least as much a positive assertion as a negative one. However, those who would go to extreme limits of simplicity are definitely in the minority. We can quite understand that our age is socially conditioned to accept, with increasing favor, the very evident trend among churches toward an enhancement of the service. It is everywhere apparent that the pendulum is swinging back again toward ritualism. The progress may be slow; the direction is significant. This significance lies in the fact that the members of our churches are expressing themselves in favor of an enlargement of the ritual. This is not something originating with the clergy. Whatever the minister is doing about it is mainly in response to the suggestions and recommendations of his people.[18]

Wide observation confirms this judgment, and it is particularly true with regard to the Communion Service.

"Reverencing" the altar and genuflection towards it are practices rarely found and not likely soon to be seen in evangelical churches, nor is one likely to observe the making of the sign of the cross in them at any time during public worship. The lack of these practices is a negative sign of distinction likely to be evident for a long time. In a great many churches of the evangelical denominations, the members of the congregation no

[17] Robert E. Keighton, *The Minister's Communion Service Book*, Judson Press, Philadelphia, 1940.

[18] Used by permission of The American Baptist Publication Society, Philadelphia.

longer bow the head for a moment of individual prayer after entering church, nor do they kneel during the offering of prayer. *O tempora! O mores!* alas! that these two most excellent customs, so long practiced by our fathers, seem no longer to be in favor.

While we are on the subject of kneeling, let it be said that the lack of sufficient room between pews, as now ordinarily placed, discourages the practice, because seating capacity has been considered first. Perhaps, too, the Puritan aversion to kneeling still exerts a lingering influence that dies hard. Kneeling promotes a pervasive feeling of reverence. God can hear our sincerely uttered prayers in any posture, but the sense of humility symbolized by kneeling is conducive to the best attitude within ourselves.

Every church with a properly furnished altar should have an Altar Guild, which should act as a special committee in charge of matters connected with the care of the altar. The women in this organization should provide the elements used in Holy Communion, see that a stock of appropriate wax candles is kept in store, look after the linens and the paraments or ornamental hangings placed about the altar, pulpit and lectern, so that everything may be done "decently and in order" and nothing essential to good order overlooked. This organization should supervise the placing of flowers upon the altar and attend to the disposition of them after use.

The proper employments of an Altar Guild furnish opportunities for an important form of lay ministry, and wherever well organized the work of the Altar Guild is quite likely to be taken care of enthusiastically.

If the church is richly symbolical in its windows and furnishings, a subcommittee of the Altar Guild can be given charge of the pleasant duty of showing and explaining the symbols to strangers after the Sunday services. Such an organization might well devote some time, at its monthly meetings, to the study of some great Christian symbol. The minister could use some member of the Guild, who has specialized in such study, as an instructor in symbolism to children undergoing preparation for entry into church membership. In any case, the work of the Altar Guild will offer a delightful form of Christian service, which is bound to appeal specially to some of the elect ladies in the church. Appropriately to its work, the meetings of the Altar Guild should always begin and end with a brief devotional period.

While we are still concerned with the altar and chancel, we will deal with the use of vestments. Surpliced choirs are now quite common in most city churches and in a good many churches in country towns. The appearance of a surpliced choir is restful to the congregation. It avoids the undesirable distraction so often caused by variety of dress in the choir. It is a contribution to simplicity of effect and concentration on worship, both much to be desired. If a surpliced choir is desirable, why not a surpliced minister? In the present unresolved state of thinking, the logical answer in most cases is not likely to be given.

In most of the evangelical churches, the use of alb, chasuble and other vestments associated with priestly

133

functions is not desired. It is said that these vestments, which are generally worn by the clergy in liturgical churches, are richly symbolical and that the use of them is supported by the twenty-eighth chapter of Exodus, in the second verse of which it is commanded: "Thou shalt make holy garments for Aaron thy brother, for glory and for beauty." Perhaps the characteristic symbolism associated with the eucharistic vestments is not, in itself, particularly objectionable. They are said to represent Christ's garments worn on Good Friday, before the crucifixion. Regarding the ordinary vestments, it is said that the cassock signifies devotion; the surplice, purity; the stole, Christ's yoke. An embroidered cope is significant of dignity of office, and so on. Any good dictionary can be consulted for further details, if wanted, and there will usually be found, close by, a group of illustrations. However, candor compels one to say that the symbolism of vestments is of comparatively late origin. It seems that most of these garments are, in fact, representative of the garments of a Roman gentleman of the third century or the early part of the fourth century. After the secular fashion changed, they were retained for ecclesiastical use. Writing of one of the most important of these, a distinguished Roman Catholic authority says that the chasuble is a secular vestment, which was elevated to the dignity of a liturgical vestment about the third century.[19]

In keeping with other characteristic attitudes assumed

[19] See Cabrol and LeClercq, *Dictionnaire d'archëologie chrétienne et de liturgie,* article "Chasuble," Vol. III. On the symbolism of vestments generally, see Walter Lowrie, *Monuments of the Early Church,* The Macmillan Co., 1901, pp. 384 ff.; *Catholic Encyclopedia,* article "Symbolism," by Herbert Thurston.

at the time of the Reformation, the reformers discarded
the extremely elaborate vestments worn by the Roman
Catholic clergy and employed the university gown of
that time for use during services of worship. So, to
this day, if a robe is used at all, the black robe of the
academic world is the one most frequently seen in the
pulpits of evangelical churches.

The wearing of a stock and neck bands, in addition
to "the Genevan gown," by Presbyterian ministers and
others, has quite generally fallen into disuse. Inciden-
tally, it should be remarked that the so-called Genevan
gown was disliked by the Genevan Puritans, who regarded it as "a priest's gown." Perhaps an academic robe
is better than a morning suit for pulpit use, but one has
to confess, regarding the former, that there is something
funereal about its unrelieved blackness.

One may be pardoned for asking, "Why should an
evangelical minister of the gospel wear an academic robe
in the pulpit?" Perhaps the answer is, "For lack of something more appropriate that church-goers will sanc-
tion." The same question can be asked concerning a
divinity hood, which is fitting for certain special occasions, such as the preaching of a baccalaureate sermon;
but, while it is very colorful, it is not particularly desirable in the pulpit, or before the altar, on ordinary occasions. Unquestionably, a divinity hood relieves the
blackness of the academic robe, and here and there one
finds this combination being used at the ordinary worship services. For the present, in the matter of pulpit
vestments, every evangelical minister is a law unto him-

135

self. This is no cause for alarm. The only danger lies in over-elaboration.

One sometimes hears the statement that the academic robe is peculiarly fitting for use in evangelical churches, because it is emblematic, in a way, of the major place given to the sermon in the services of such churches. In the days of two- and three-hour sermons, that was a cogent plea. However, in this day of widespread higher education and desire for emphasis on corporate worship the sermon is no longer generally expected to be a sort of intellectual *tour de force*. Everywhere, there is a revival of interest in corporate worship as the supreme means of securing spiritual benefit in public services. This trend can be observed in the churches of many evangelical denominations.[20]

Beyond challenge stands the truth that a richly symbolical church structure and richly symbolical forms of worship will avail nothing unless the presence and the power of the Holy Spirit are felt in the lives of the worshipers. This is not said by way of disparagement of a place of worship which, like the Jewish temple of old, is made glorious for the feet of God. Nor is it so said of solemn and beautiful forms of approach to his Presence. It is intended to call to mind that it is only the fruitful issue of it all in men's daily conduct that counts for the purification of societal life, as well as for the promotion of the spiritual welfare of "the beloved community," the church itself.

[20] Von Ogden Vogt, *Modern Worship*, Yale University Press, 1927; p. 151. *Also* Andrew Blackwood, *The Fine Art of Public Worship*, Cokesbury Press, 1939, p. 221.

CHAPTER XI

Symbolism of Color

IN THOSE CHURCHES which observe the Christian Year closely, it is customary to change the color of the paraments or ornamental hangings upon the altar, pulpit and lectern in accordance with the season. Color is used as a sign of the mood of a church festival. For those who may be interested in knowing something about the plan of color variation and its meaning, a brief description is given.

The accepted ecclesiastical interpretation of color is as follows:

Green, being usually the most evident color in nature, is regarded as the universal color. It is symbolical of hope, also of growth in the Christian life.

Red symbolizes blood, fire, Christian zeal, the work and ministry of the Church.

White (or *White and Gold*) signifies purity, light, rejoicing, the Godhead.

Black signifies mourning.

Purple or *Violet* signifies penitence, watching, fasting.

There is considerable difference between the Lutheran, Reformed, Anglican, Roman and Eastern Orthodox bodies in the employment of color, not to speak of variations within the same body. Therefore, the following outline is only a general guide and those desiring more particular information will need to consult the proper denominational authority or official calendar.

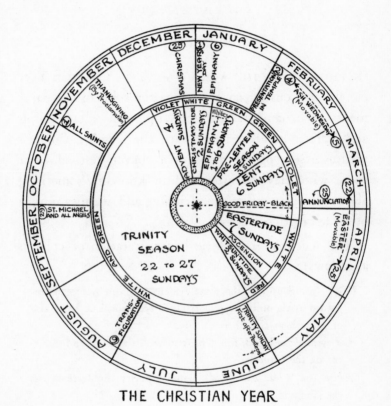

THE CHRISTIAN YEAR

White is the proper color for seasons relating to Jesus, particularly for Christmas, Epiphany Day, Easter Sunday, and Trinity Sunday. White is also used at weddings.

Red should be used at Pentecost, also at the dedica-

138

tion of a church, or at an anniversary of its founding; likewise, for Thanksgiving Day.

Black is the color for Good Friday; also at funeral services and on days of humiliation and prayer in connection with catastrophe.

Purple or violet should be used throughout the forty days of Lent, except on Good Friday. However, this plan may be varied by using white during the first four weeks of Lent, red during the fifth week, and black during the last week.

Green is generally used during the seasons of Epiphany and Trinity.

If a church does not desire or cannot afford more than one altar cloth, it should be red, because red is significant of the work and ministry of the Church universal.

It seems that the early Christian Church followed the color system of the Jewish Temple; namely, red, white, and blue, and these colors were retained in the Church of England, until a couple of hundred years before the Reformation, when Roman influence made a more elaborate system popular. The British national colors, and in turn the American, were derived from the old English ecclesiastical color scheme, in which red prevailed. Increasingly, the non-liturgical evangelical denominations are giving attention to the seasons of the Christian Year, while retaining a large degree of freedom and informality in worship.

A LIFE OF CHRIST IN SYMBOLS
(PLATE II)

CHAPTER XII

Teaching Christian Symbolism

FROM HIS PREVIOUS experience in publishing a small devotional manual to be given to persons at the time of joining the church,[1] the author discovered that there is extraordinary interest in Christian symbolism in the churches today. The booklet mentioned contains only twenty of the great Christian symbols, yet this feature has attracted widespread interest.

Under present-day conditions, the instruction of children preparatory to being received into full membership in the church often is a hurried and sketchy affair. Abstractions are notoriously difficult of retention by the average mind. Some sort of visual aid must be employed in order to secure more satisfactory results. A business man told the author recently that the only thing that remained in his memory out of the course of training which he received for church membership, was the explanation of certain great Christian symbols on the walls and in the windows of the church. This case is not singular. Therefore, pastors would be well advised to supplement the ordinary brief preparatory course with one in Christian symbolism. More than likely, it will soon be found that this supplementary course is really of basic importance.

[1] *Guide-Marks on the Christian Way*, Abingdon-Cokesbury Press.

In the First Methodist Church, Evanston, Illinois, not only are visitors shown its extraordinary wealth of symbolism, but children in training for church membership are conducted around the church and chapel and instructed as thoroughly as possible in the significance of the symbols. This church has an unusually beautiful chapel (*see frontispiece*), on the walls of which the stonecutters incised a series of symbols concerning the life of Christ.

Since this series, as a whole, has much merit, a fairly representative sketch of it is presented in Plate N. Most of the panels may be interpreted easily by anyone after perusing the previous chapters of this book, but perhaps a little additional explanation of the figures is in order:

(1) The lily, signifying the Annunciation; (2) the Star of Epiphany; (3) the visit of three wise men from the east, supposed to be kings who found the Holy Child at Bethlehem; also the flight into Egypt, symbolized by the sun disk, asps[2] and wings; (4) the offering of doves for sacrifice;[3] (5) the baptism at the Jordan by John the Baptist, the wavy lines suggesting the flowing water; (6) the Temptation in which the devil took Jesus up into a high mountain and offered him "all the kingdoms of the world" in exchange for an act of worship; (7) the Sermon on the Mount, symbolized by a mountain with the Christogram *XP* on it; the waves of near-by Lake Galilee being represented in the foreground; (8) the Transfiguration symbolized by two

[2] Sometimes called "Uraei."
[3] Luke 2:24.

142

tables of stone for Moses, a burning chariot wheel for Elijah, and the *IHC* monogram for Jesus—the three representing, respectively, the Law, the Prophets and the Gospel; (9) the palm leaves signifying the Triumphal Entry into Jerusalem; (10) the chalice and wafer signifying the institution of the Lord's Supper; [4] (11) the cup of submission and the pointed Cross of Agony, surrounded by olive leaves signifying the Garden of Gethsemane; (12) the purse and thirty pieces of silver, emblematic of the betrayal of Christ by Judas; (13) the cock crowing, signifying Peter's denial of his Lord; (14) the axe, fasces and scales with the initials "S.P.Q.R.," standing for the Latin phrase *Senatus Populusque Romanus;* [5] the scales, out of balance, signifying the unjust trial of Jesus under Pontius Pilate; (15) the crown of thorns signifying the torture of Jesus, and the three nails used for the crucifixion; (16) the veil of the Temple rent in twain, revealing the three crosses on Calvary; (17) the phoenix, legendary bird signifying Christ's resurrection; (18) the Cross of Christ triumphant over the world.

Instruction on this significant series of symbols, representing the life and work of Christ, can be expanded at the will of the instructor; and perhaps it will be appreciated more than any other feature of the course of training.

[4] Matt. 26.

[5] The word *Populus-que* must be divided as indicated in order to obtain the initials "P.Q." The phrase means "the Senate and the Roman People." In combination with the axe and fasces, these initials symbolized the authority of the Roman State.

THE SACRAMENTS AND THE CHRISTIAN LIFE
(PLATE O)

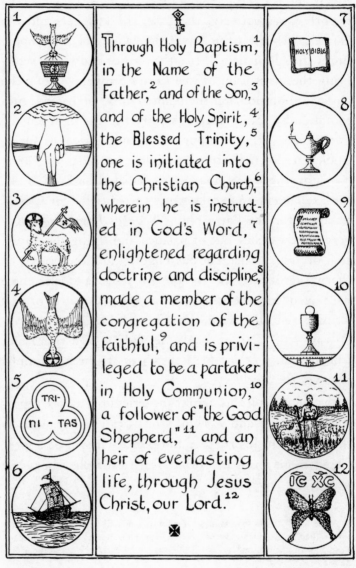

Through Holy Baptism,[1] in the Name of the Father,[2] and of the Son,[3] and of the Holy Spirit,[4] the Blessed Trinity,[5] one is initiated into the Christian Church,[6] wherein he is instructed in God's Word,[7] enlightened regarding doctrine and discipline,[8] made a member of the congregation of the faithful,[9] and is privileged to be a partaker in Holy Communion,[10] a follower of "the Good Shepherd,"[11] and an heir of everlasting life, through Jesus Christ, our Lord.[12]

Furthermore, in Plate O will be found interesting materials which can be used as a basis of instruction on the Sacraments and Christian life. Because of the consecutive interpretation in the center panel of the plate and the explanations of the various symbols previously given in this book, very little more is necessary.

Figure 1 is a common symbol of Christian Baptism—the Holy Spirit as a dove descending toward a font with the Christogram on it. Figure 9 is a scroll signifying church membership. Figure 10 is a chalice and wafer appearing on an altar and signifying Holy Communion. Figure 11 represents Christ as "the Good Shepherd." Figure 12—the butterfly—denotes immortality, coupled with a Greek contraction signifying "Jesus Christ." The material in the chapter on "Symbolism on the Great Chalice of Antioch" can be utilized also to show how the precious symbolism of the Lord's Supper was kept in constant remembrance in the early Christian Church.

In the illustration on page 147 we have a picture of a beautiful reredos cross carved in oak. The grouping of symbols in it is interesting and instructive. This cross is "a Tree of Life" symbolizing the words of our Lord: "I am the vine, ye are the branches." [6] Intertwined in the branches are the symbols of the leading apostles, reading right to left downward continuously, as follows:

ST. PETER: two keys saltier.
ST. PAUL: a sword.
ST. JUDE: a sail boat.
ST. JAMES THE LESS: a saw.

[6] John 15:5.

145

St. James the Greater: a scallop shell.
St. Andrew: an X-like cross.
St. Philip: a slender cross and two loaves.
St. Thomas: a vertical spear and a carpenter's square.

The symbols of the Four Evangelists are placed at the ends of the cross, a customary method of placing them on large crosses. They appear as follows:

Top—St. John: a winged eagle.
Left arm—St. Matthew: a winged man.
Right arm—St. Mark: a winged lion.
Below—St. Luke: a winged ox.

At the intersection of Tree and crossbeam appears the *XP* monogram surrounded by a circular aureole, signifying the glory of the risen and ascended Christ.

Such an impressive treasure of modern Christian art within a church is an ever-eloquent testimonial of the power of the Gospel of Jesus Christ, enabling men to endure perils by land and sea, and to die as martyrs with unflinching faith in their Lord.

On page 148 there is a picture of the altar and reredos in the sanctuary of the First Methodist Church, Evanston, Illinois. The reredos of carved oak is one of the finest in this country. It was designed by the distinguished architect, Ralph Adams Cram, and the carving was executed by the firm of Irving and Casson, Boston, Massachusetts. It is a remarkable example of beauty and teaching in the sanctuary.

In the principal panel, center top, appears the figure of the risen Christ, emerging from the tomb, his head surrounded by a tri-radiant nimbus, his body surrounded

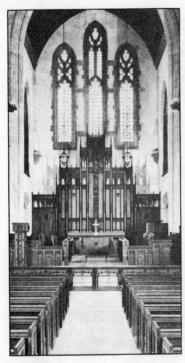

Left: NAVE AND CHANCEL, FIRST METHODIST CHURCH, WILMETTE, ILLINOIS.

Right: "TREE OF LIFE" CROSS; DETAIL FROM THE CENTRAL PANEL OF THE REREDOS; DESIGN BY FRANK L. VENNING; CARVING BY ALOIS LANG.

Courtesy of American Seating Company, Grand Rapids, Michigan.

147

ALTAR AND REREDOS, FIRST METHODIST CHURCH, EVANSTON,
ILLINOIS

by an aureole with rays indicative of glory, his right hand raised in benediction, his left hand holding the staff from which flies the pennant of Victory. Immediately below his feet, on the left, is represented the angel who rolled away the stone that sealed the tomb and, on the right, the Roman soldier who fell asleep while on guard at the tomb.

At the bottom of the principal panel, Christ is shown in the Garden of Gethsemane, with the three sleeping disciples in the background, and an angel, in the upper right-hand corner, represented as witnessing the Passion.

Left, top to bottom, we see (1) the shepherds visiting the Holy Child in the stable at Bethlehem; (2) the baptism of Jesus in the river Jordan by John the Baptist, the Holy Spirit appearing in the form of a descending dove; (3) the healing of the man sick with the palsy.

Right, top to bottom, shows (1) Christ preaching the Sermon on the Mount; (2) the Transfiguration, with Jesus in the center; Moses on the right, bearing the two tables of stone, representing the Law; Elijah on the left, representing the Prophets; Peter, James and John in the foreground in an attitude of adoration; (3) the crucifixion, with Mary, the Mother of our Lord, and John, the disciple, standing by the cross. At the top, in the center, two angels support a shield on which is carved a ship, symbolic of the Christian Church. Down both sides, adoring angels are represented in various postures.

The pairs of small figures, outlining the panels, represent the prophetic voices of the ages. On the left, in

149

descending order, going from left to right, are (1) Origen and Luther; (2) Saint Peter and Saint Augustine; (3) Isaiah and Amos. On the right, in descending order, going from left to right: (1) John Calvin and John Wesley; (2) Saint Francis of Assisi and Saint Paul; (3) Jeremiah and Saint Thomas Aquinas. The altar cross is of the Latin type, but it has a small Greek cross at the center of the intersection. Since the photograph was taken, the altar cross has been set on a small retable. An ornamental cross, with arms of equal length, is incised on the front of the altar, in the center panel.

APPENDIX

Bibliography

BOOKLETS

BEAVER, R. PIERCE. *The House of God*. St. Louis: Eden Publishing Co., 1935.

BURDICK, MARJORIE J. *Church Symbolism*. Boston: Chapman and Grimes, 1940.

KUNKLE, H. R. *Symbols and Terms of the Church*. Philadelphia: United Lutheran Publishing House, 1938.

WILSON, BISHOP FRANK E. *An Outline of Christian Symbolism*. Milwaukee: Morehouse, 1933.

WILSON, BISHOP FRANK E. *An Outline of The Christian Year*. Milwaukee: Morehouse, 1941.

JUVENILE BOOKS

BAINTON, ROLAND H. *The Church of Our Fathers*. New York: Scribner's, 1941. Church History and Symbolism combined.

BROOKMAN, ALICE M. *"My Own" Workbook on Christian Symbolism*. New York: Morehouse-Gorham, 1940.

GRIFFITH, HELEN S. *The Sign Language of Our Faith*. Washington, D. C.: St. Alban's Press, 1939.

LEACHMAN, E. W. *The Church's Object Lessons*. London: Mowbray, 1919.

BOOKS FOR ARCHITECTS, ARTISTS AND STUDENTS OF CHRISTIAN ART

AUDSLEY, WM. AND G. A. *A Handbook of Christian Symbolism*. London: Day, 1865.

BAILEY, H. T. AND ETHEL POOL. *Symbolism for Artists*. Worcester, Mass.: Davis Press, 1925.

DE BLES, MAJOR A. *How to Distinguish the Saints in Art*. New York: Art Culture Publications, 1925.

GOLDSMITH, ELISABETH. *Sacred Symbols in Art*. New York: Putnam's, 1912.

SMITH, H. J. *Symbols of the Jewish, Greek, Latin and Modern Churches.* Philadelphia: 1900.

WEBBER, F. R. *Church Symbolism.* Cleveland: Jansen, 1938. Copiously illustrated.

BOOKS ON SYMBOLISM AND SYMBOLICS

ALLEN, J. R. *Early Christian Symbols in Great Britain and Ireland.* London: 1887.

BEVAN, EDWYN R. *Symbolism and Belief.* New York: The Macmillan Co., 1938.

BRIGGS, C. A. *Theological Symbolics.* New York: Scribner's, 1914. Volume in International Theological Library series.

D'ALVIELLA, G. *The Migration of Symbols.* London: 1894.

DIDRON, ADOLPHE N. *Christian Iconography.* Paris: 1845.

DURANDUS, BISHOP. *The Symbolism of Churches, Etc.* (Translation.) London: 1893.

EVANS, E. P. *Animal Symbolism in Ecclesiastical Architecture.* New York: Henry Holt, 1896.

FLEMING, D. J. *Christian Symbols in a World Community.* New York: Friendship Press, 1940.

GOLDSMITH, ELISABETH. *Ancient Pagan Symbols.* New York: Putnam's, 1929.

HULME, F. *History, Principles and Practice of Symbolism.* London: 1889.

JAMESON, MRS. ANNA B. *Sacred and Legendary Art.* 2 vols. London: 1870.

KLOTSCHE, E. H. *Christian Symbolics.* Burlington, Ia.: Lutheran Literary Board, 1929.

MACKENZIE, DONALD A. *The Migration of Symbols.* New York: Knopf, 1926.

NEFF, ELIZABETH C. *An Anglican Study in Christian Symbolism.* Cleveland: The Helman-Taylor Co., 1898.

ROLFE, C. C. *The Ancient Use of Liturgical Colours.* London: 1879.

STRYZGOWSKI, J. *Origin of Christian Church Art.* Oxford: 1923.

BIBLIOGRAPHY

Twining, Louisa. *Symbols and Emblems of Early and Medieval Christian Art*. London: John Murray, 1885.

BOOKS ON OTHER SUBJECTS, BUT HAVING A BEARING ON CHRISTIAN SYMBOLISM

Bennett, Charles W. *Christian Archeology*. New York: Eaton and Mains, 1898.

Blackwood, Andrew. *The Fine Art of Public Worship*. Nashville: Cokesbury Press, 1939.

Brilioth, Yngve. *Eucharistic Faith and Practice in Evangelical and Catholic Churches*. Translated by A. G. Hebert. New York: The Macmillan Co., 1934.

Bumpus, John S. *A Dictionary of Ecclesiastical Terms*. London: Laurie (no date).

Clarke, W. K. L. *Liturgy and Worship*. London: S.P.C.K., 1932.

Hapgood, I. F. (Translator). *Service Book of the Eastern Orthodox Church* (Russian). New York: Association Press, 1906, chapter on "Symbolism."

Harmon, N. B., Jr. *The Rites and Ritual of Episcopal Methodism*. Nashville: Cokesbury Press, 1926.

Hebert, A. G. *Liturgy and Society*. London: Faber and Faber, 1935.

Lowrie, Walter. *Monuments of the Early Church*. New York: The Macmillan Co., 1901.

Lundy, J. P. *Monumental Christianity*. New York: 1876.

Palmer, Albert W. *The Art of Conducting Public Worship*. New York: The Macmillan Co., 1939.

Parkhurst, Helen H. *Cathedral*. Boston: Houghton Mifflin, 1936, chapter on "Symbolism."

Prentice, Sartell. *The Heritage of the Cathedral*. New York: Morrow, 1936.

Prentice, Sartell. *The Voices of the Cathedral*. New York: Morrow. 1938.

Richardson, Norman E. *Toward a More Efficient Church* (published privately), 1940. A Manual in use at the Presbyterian Theological Seminary, Chicago, which contains a good many pages of accurately drawn symbols and a great variety of helps for pastors who mimeograph their own church bulletins.

SEIDENSPINNER, CLARENCE. *Form and Freedom in Worship.* Chicago: Willett, Clark & Co., 1941.

SMITH AND CHEETHAM. *Dictionary of Christian Antiquities.* Hartford, Conn.: Burr, 1880.

STRODACH, P. Z. *A Manual on Worship.* Philadelphia: United Lutheran Publishing House, 1930.

THURSTON, HERBERT. *The Catholic Encyclopedia.* Article on "Symbolism."

N.B.—*Christian Symbolism,* by F. R. Webber, contains a very extensive bibliography listing many books now out of print, access to which can be obtained only in large public libraries or the libraries of theological seminaries. This is also true of a few of the titles listed in this bibliography.

Definitions of Church Terms and Usages [1]

ADVENT—The season which begins the Christian Year by commemorating the coming of Christ. It includes the four Sundays before Christmas.

ALTAR—A raised structure, of stone or wood, within the chancel of a church, having a "Mensa," or table, on which is usually placed the vessels, etc., used during administration of the Lord's Supper or Holy Communion. It is in the most prominent place in the church. It is commonly raised the height of three steps above the floor on which it stands, these steps serving as a reminder that faith, hope and love are requisite to proper reception of the memorial elements which signify the sacrifice of Christ. Ordinarily, an altar bears a cross and two candles, one on either side of the cross, the cross signifying the triumph of Christ over death and sin, and the candles, when lighted, signifying that He is "the Light of the World."

AMEN—A Hebrew word meaning "true," "certain." It is derived from *aman*, meaning "to strengthen." It is usually uttered at the end of a prayer, in the sense of "So be it!" Sung at the ends of hymns, it is of variable value, sometimes meaning little more than a sort of musical "full stop."

ANTIPHONAL—Responsive; referring to responsive reading, singing or chanting.

ASCENSION DAY—The fortieth day after Easter, observed in commemoration of Christ's Ascension to the Right Hand of God. Also called Holy Thursday.

ASH WEDNESDAY—The first day of the penitential season known as Lent. Its name is derived from the practice in Catholic churches of marking the foreheads of the penitents with ashes, while the priest says: "Remember, O man, that thou art dust and to dust

[1] A good many terms in this list are not used, or are seldom used in evangelical churches. However, they are inserted for the sake of information, or for the purpose of pointing out contrast between various usages.

157

thou shalt return." The day is now observed by a good many evangelical churches, but without the ceremony just described.

BISHOP—This word is derived from the Greek and means "overseer." A bishop is a clergyman who has been consecrated or ordained as a chief pastor, and usually appointed or elected to serve as the spiritual head and business administrator of a designated diocese, district or area of his Church. In the Anglican Church and related bodies, ordination as a bishop elevates a clergyman to a third order, ranking above priests and deacons. The Presbyterian churches have only one ministerial order, that of presbyter or elder. In the Roman Catholic Church, a bishop is a priest consecrated and given authority to administer the sacraments of Ordination and Confirmation. His orders are not higher than those of a priest, but the powers which he can exercise are more extensive. In line with John Wesley's opinions about primitive Christian orders, American Methodists regard the bishopric as an office and not an order. In the past, they have used both "ordain" and "consecrate" with reference to the ceremony of setting a minister apart for the work of the episcopacy. Apparently, the distinction between bishop and presbyter was not sharply drawn in sub-apostolic times.[1] *See* PRIEST; *also* ORDINATION.

CANTICLE—A hymn taken from the Holy Scriptures and arranged for chanting in public worship.

CASSOCK—The long, black, foundation vestment worn by members of the choir and, in certain liturgical churches, by the priest and by the person who assists him in the celebration of Holy Communion.

CATECHUMEN—A person who is undergoing instruction in the elements of the Christian religion, with a view to entering the membership of the church.

CATHEDRAL—From the Greek *cathedra*, meaning "a seat." A cathedral is so called solely because it contains the chair or seat of the bishop of the diocese. The word is often used wrongly in ref-

---

[1] The *"Didache,"* a document said to date from the first half of the second century, in Section 15, speaks of bishops and deacons (*episcopous kai diakonous*), omitting reference to presbyters, which would lead to the inference that bishops and presbyters exercised similar functions.

erence to a great church structure, even in denominations which have no bishops. A true cathedral might be a small church.

CATHOLIC—This is a word of Greek origin, in its generic sense meaning "universal." In that sense it was used with reference to the Christian Church in the Apostles' Creed. Since the complete separation of the Western Church from the Eastern, in A.D. 1054, as the result of a dispute over the use of images, it has been customary to speak of the Western Church as the Roman Catholic Church and more fully as "The Holy Catholic Apostolic Roman Church"; the Eastern Church being known as the Orthodox Church or, more particularly, as "The Holy Orthodox Catholic Apostolic Church." In evangelical usage, the word "catholic" refers to those, in all churches, who are true followers of Jesus Christ. John 10:16 favors this interpretation, which is believed to be more in keeping with the original meaning than a delimited definition applicable to one or a few denominational bodies. In contrast to the evangelical view, Roman Catholics put tradition on an equal footing with the Holy Scriptures as a source of doctrines. All "Catholics" insist upon holding the doctrine of uninterrupted episcopal succession from the apostles to the present time. Indeed, this doctrine is a distinguishing characteristic of "Catholicity," as the term is now used. *See* EVANGELICAL.

CHALICE—From the Latin *calix,* meaning "a cup." It is the cup which holds the wine consecrated and used during Holy Communion.

CHANCEL—In general, the part of the church which contains the altar, the pulpit, the lectern and the choir stalls or seats. *See* SANCTUARY.

CHANCEL RAIL—The rail, balustrade, or parapet, which divides the chancel from the remainder of the church.

CHOIR—The part of the chancel reserved for singers; also the singers.

CHOIR STALLS—The seats provided for the singers in cruciform churches, usually arranged in two groups, one on each side of the approach to the altar, an arrangement adapted to antiphonal singing.

CHRISTIAN YEAR—In liturgical churches, the program of

church activity is intimately connected with the Christian Year, which is divided into eight seasons as follows: Advent; Christmas; Epiphany; Lent; Easter, Ascensiontide; Whitsuntide; Trinity. There are a good many special days of which the more important are: Saint Andrew's Day; Circumcision; Good Friday; Transfiguration; All Saints' Day. In accord with the seasons as indicated in the church calendar, an appropriately varied color scheme, for regulating the use of paraments and vestments, has been established. The use of color for symbolic purposes, in the Christian Church, is ancient, being relatively simple in the early centuries and quite elaborate in later times.

CHRISTMAS—The festival of the Nativity of our Lord. Gifts are associated with it, because of the gifts brought to Bethlehem by "the wise men from the east." Christmas was not celebrated until the fourth century. At first, January 6 was chosen, but later, December 25 was substituted to avoid confusion with the celebration of the Baptism of Jesus on January 6. December 25 was probably selected because of the Roman festival on that date celebrating the time of the winter solstice. The true birthdate is unknown, but doubtless the Christians avoided invidious attention from their pagan neighbors by celebrating the Advent of Christ on a day of general festival.

CLERGY STALLS—The seats for the ministers in the chancel, near the pulpit and the lectern respectively. They are sometimes called "sedilia."

COLLECT—A brief prayer, on a single subject, usually divided into five parts: the address, the ground of the petition, the petition proper, the benefit desired, and the meditation. A "Collect" nearly always ends with the words, "through Jesus Christ, our Lord." The origin of the word "Collect" is uncertain. It seems that in medieval times it used to be the custom in Rome for a group of the clergy to collect at a certain central place and go in procession from there to a previously chosen church, for the purpose of celebration of the Mass. It is said that "Collect" was the name given to the brief prayer offered at the point of collection or assembly. Others think that the word refers to a collection of prayer ideas.

160

Again, by others, it is contended that originally it was the prayer said over the congregation when all were collected.

COTTA—From a late Latin word meaning "coat," a short surplice. *See* SURPLICE.

CREDENCE—A small table, or wall-bracket, usually placed at the right of the altar, for the purpose of holding the elements to be consecrated in Holy Communion; also, the offering plates and the Service Book.

CRUCIFIX—A cross bearing the likeness of the body of Christ, usually thorn-crowned and having the appearance of suffering. The crucifix is not favored for altar use in most evangelical churches. The empty cross, symbolizing Christ's triumph over death, is preferred.

DEACON—This term is derived from the Greek *diakonis*, meaning "a servant." It refers to the lowest major order of the ministry in the Protestant Episcopal Church. In non-episcopal churches, it refers to a church's secular officer, who assists the minister in certain of his duties and looks after business concerns of the church. In The Methodist Church in the United States, a deacon is an ordained minister who can perform ministerial functions, except administration of the sacrament of the Lord's Supper in which he is permitted to assist an elder. In Catholic churches, the duties of the deacons are mainly liturgical.

DOSSAL, DOSSEL, DORSAL—The ornate wall curtain or screen placed behind and above the altar. *See* REREDOS.

EASTER—The word "Easter" is derived from the Anglo-Saxon *Eastre,* the goddess of Spring and Dawn. Easter is the greatest and oldest festival of the Christian Church. It commemorates our Lord's resurrection from the dead. This festival was not observed in apostolic times and was established only after bitter controversy in the second and third centuries regarding the date. It is known as a "movable feast" and falls upon the Sunday following the full moon which appears on, or next after, the Spring equinox.

ELDER—This word is the English equivalent of the Greek word *presbyteros,* from which the word "priest" is derived by contraction. In those churches which recognize two ministerial orders, "elder" means a fully qualified minister ranking above a deacon.

In a good many non-liturgical churches, the word "elder" is the equivalent of and the substitute for "priest." In the Anglican Church and related bodies, a priest ranks between a deacon (the lowest order) and a bishop. The priesthood is one of three "major" holy orders in the Roman Catholic Church, the members of the hierarchy which rank above the priests having superior powers but not superior orders.

ELEMENTS—The bread and wine used in Holy Communion.

EPIPHANY—The Christian festival which commemorates the manifestation of Christ to "the wise men," representing the Gentile world. The date is January 6, or the twelfth day after Christmas.

EPISTLE-SIDE—The right side of the altar, as the congregation faces it; so called because in liturgical churches the epistle for the day is read at that side of the altar. See GOSPEL-SIDE.

EUCHARIST—A liturgical name for Holy Communion or the Lord's Supper. The word has reference to thanksgiving. In the early Church, celebration of the Lord's Supper usually began with offering thanks to God. Although it is a beautiful word, its use is not favored by evangelicals, because of sacerdotal connotations. See SACERDOTAL.

EVANGELICAL—The type of Christianity which emphasizes the authority of the Holy Scriptures rather than the authority of the Church. The name is derived from the Evangelists who wrote the four Gospels, which contain most of the teachings of Jesus. Evangelicals deny the right of the Church to develop new dogmas which cannot be clearly derived or inferred from the teachings of the Bible. They regard Holy Communion as a symbolic, memorial service, at which Christ is present only in a spiritual sense.[2] Christian Baptism is regarded by most of them as symbolic of cleansing from sin, but not actually regenerative in its effect. They recognize these two sacraments and no others. As a consequence of their views on the sacraments, their concept of the ministry differs radically from the Roman Catholic concept. See CATHOLIC; also SACERDOTAL.

[2] Lutherans hold that there is a real "sacramental presence," "in, with and under" the "elements," but do not regard it as the result of a sacerdotal act of the minister.

GARTH—An enclosed garden, or courtyard, within a cloister or surrounded by the buildings of a church; a cathedral close.

GLORIA PATRI—The "Glory to the Father," sometimes called "the lesser Doxology." An ascription of praise usually sung at worship services, after reading from the Psalter. The words are the first two occurring in the full Latin ascription, which reads: *Gloria Patri, et Filio, et Spiritui Sancto, sicut erat in principio et nunc et semper, et in saecula saeculorum. Amen.*

GOOD FRIDAY—The most solemn day of the Christian Year, observed by all Christians in commemoration of the death of Christ on the cross. It always falls on the Friday preceding Easter Sunday. *See* EASTER.

GOSPEL-SIDE—The left side of the altar as the congregation faces it; so called because in liturgical churches the gospel for the day is read at that side of the altar. *See* EPISTLE-SIDE.

GRADINE—A shelf, or one of the shelves, placed at the back of an altar on which candlesticks and the cross are placed. *See* RETABLE.

HOLY WEEK—The week before Easter.

INTINCTION—The practice of administering the elements in the sacrament of Holy Communion by dipping the bread (wafer) in the wine so that both can be given together. Only a part of the wafer is thus dipped. This method is standard practice in the Eastern Orthodox Church. Under certain conditions, this practice is permitted by the Protestant Episcopal Church. However, it has been condemned on the ground that it appears to deny the cup to the laity.

INTROIT—From the Latin *introitus*, meaning "an entering," the appointed psalm for the day read immediately preceding the commencement of the Holy Communion in the liturgical churches. In other churches, it is an introductory piece sung or chanted at the beginning of a worship service.

JESSE-WINDOW—A design in a stained glass window, representing the tree of Christ's descent from Jesse, the father of David.

KNEELER—A low bench placed conveniently in pews for kneeling. "Hassock" is the term applied to an individual cushion for the same purpose.

163

KYRIE or KYRIE ELEISON—"Lord, have mercy upon us," an ancient Greek litany, probably of Hebrew origin, found in nearly all rituals for administration of Holy Communion. In the Roman Catholic Mass, it follows the Introit. In liturgical churches, it is generally chanted in ninefold recitation during celebration of the Eucharist. In such usage, the three middle petitions are changed to "Christ, have mercy upon us," *Christe eleison*. As heard in the Liturgy of the Eastern Orthodox Church, it is very impressive.

LECTERN—The reading desk from which the Scripture lessons are read at worship services.

LECTIONARY—A collection of readings, usually from the Holy Scriptures, for use in public services of worship.

LENT—From the Anglo-Saxon *lengten*, meaning Spring, referring to lengthening days. It is a penitential season, beginning with Ash Wednesday and lasting forty days in commemoration of Christ's fast and temptation in the wilderness.[3] It is used as a period of spiritual self-discipline in preparation for Easter, and is widely observed in evangelical churches. It is a period of prescribed fasting in all Catholic churches.

LITANY—From the Greek *litaneia*, meaning "prayer." A solemn form of supplication consisting of brief petitions uttered by the minister and the congregation. For examples, *see Book of Common Prayer*. This form of prayer was first used as a processional prayer, in times of severe epidemic sickness (fifth century).

LITANY DESK—Sometimes called *"prie-dieu,"* the prayer desk at which the minister kneels in the nave, facing the altar, when he joins his people in recitation of the brief penitential, intercessory prayers known as the Litany.

LITURGY—From the Greek *leiton*, meaning "public," and *ergon*, meaning "work" or "service."[4] In its ecclesiastical sense, it means the prescribed forms of public worship of a church. The Eastern Orthodox Churches use the more definitive expression "Divine Liturgy." In its most restricted sense, the word Liturgy applies particularly to the ritual for the celebration of Holy

[3] Matt. 4:2.
[4] The Greek term from which our word "liturgy" is derived was used, in New Testament times, for any kind of public work, such as tax-gathering, police service, etc.

Communion, which is regarded as the heart of the Liturgy in all Catholic churches.[5]

MASS—Among Catholics, this is a common name for Holy Communion and is derived from one of the words of dismissal at the end of the Roman Eucharistic ritual: *Ite, missa est,* meaning, "Go, dismissal is made." (For detailed studies of the Mass and similar rites, see the two books mentioned in footnote 5.) The word mass is the last syllable of such words as Christmas (Christ-mass), Candlemas (candle-mass), Childermas (children's-mass).

MAUNDY THURSDAY—The Thursday of Holy Week, kept in commemoration of the institution of Holy Communion by our Lord. It is sometimes called "the Day of Footwashing," in allusion to the ancient custom of washing the feet of certain persons, a practice still observed in a limited way in remembrance of our Lord's washing of the feet of his disciples. The reigning monarch of England formerly was expected to perform this ceremony and distribute gifts to the poor. The custom of distributing the gifts is still maintained by English royalty. Apparently, the word "maundy" is derived from the Latin *mandatum,* an order, referring to the command given in John 13:5, 14, 34, when Jesus washed the feet of his disciples.

MENSA—The top or table of an altar.

MINISTER—A clergyman authorized to preach, administer the sacraments, and serve a parish as a cure of souls. It is a much more inclusive word than PREACHER, which is often used carelessly, as if it were exactly synonymous with MINISTER. *See* PREACHER; *also* PASTOR.

MISSAL—A liturgical book containing the Roman Catholic Ritual for Mass throughout the Christian Year.

NARTHEX—An architectural term for the vestibule of a church (see page 109 for explanation of the historic background of this interesting word).

NAVE—The part of a cruciform church in which most of the

[5] For detailed information, *see* W. K. Lowther Clarke, *Liturgy and Worship,* S.P.C.K., London, 1932; *also* Yngve Brilioth, *Eucharistic Faith and Practice in Evangelical and Catholic Churches* (translated by A. G. Hebert), The Macmillan Co., New York, 1934.

congregation is seated. It reaches from the chancel to the ecclesiastical "west end" of the church.

NIMBUS—In Christian art, a circle or cloud of light, placed around a head or a figure, representing a divine person or a saint. It is derived from a Latin word meaning "cloud." It is preferable to the word "halo," which is not a proper ecclesiastical term.

OBLATION—From the Latin *ob*, meaning "against," and *latus*, meaning "to bring." It signifies the bringing or offering of a sacrifice. Used especially with reference to the bread and wine of the Eucharist. In the early Church, bread, wine and gifts were brought by each of the communicants. The word applies to the act of offering, as well as to that which is offered. It is used in the ritual for administration of Holy Communion in some evangelical churches and particularly at the consecration of the elements.

OFFERING—The bringing of gifts as an act of worship. It is a much better word than "collection," which does not imply giving with worshipful intent.

OFFERTORY—In evangelical churches, the musical selection rendered at the time the offering is taken. In liturgical churches, the verse of a Psalm or other portion of Holy Scripture said by the priest, or sung by the choir, during the offering of the bread and wine in Holy Communion.

ORDINATION—In the Roman Catholic Church, a sacrament conferring an order; for example, that of priest or deacon. In the evangelical churches, ordination is more of an act of consecration than of conferring power. While it gives authority to administer sacraments, it is not claimed that sacerdotal power is transmitted. *See* SACERDOTAL.

ORIENTATION—In liturgical churches, the act of the priest in turning towards the altar or ecclesiastical "east" for those parts of the service in which he speaks to God for the people. In the majority of evangelical churches, the act of orientation is seldom seen, except when the plates containing the offering are placed on the altar, with a prayer of dedication. The word literally means "turning to the east."

PALM SUNDAY—The Sunday before Easter, which commemorates the triumphal entry of Christ into Jerusalem. On this occasion, branches of palm trees were strewn in the roadway by the multitude.

PARAMENTS—The name usually given to cloths used to adorn the altar, pulpit and lectern.

PARISH—From the Greek *paroikia*, meaning "a neighborhood." An ecclesiastical district assigned to the oversight and care of one clergyman.

PASCH—The Jewish Passover. The term is used sometimes for Easter.

PASCHAL LAMB—The lamb which was slain and eaten at the Jewish Passover.

PASTOR—A word meaning "shepherd." Some denominational bodies prefer this word rather than "minister." However, as commonly employed with regard to religious work, "pastor" and "minister" are closely related in scope of meaning.

PATEN—From the Latin *patena*, meaning "a pan." It is the plate used for distribution of the consecrated bread in the Communion Service.

PENTECOST—The Seventh Sunday after Easter, kept in commemoration of the descent of the Holy Spirit upon the Apostles in the form of tongues of fire. Pentecost is also known as Whitsunday. Pentecost means "fiftieth." Jewish Pentecost was kept the fiftieth day after the second day of the Passover. *See* WHITSUNDAY.

PLAINSONG—Singing of a droning, recitative character used in the Christian Church from early times and still in use in liturgical churches.

PRAYER DESK—Sometimes called *"prie-dieu"* (French: meaning "pray-God"). A small kneeling desk for use by the clergy in liturgical churches. *See* LITANY DESK.

PREACHER—A much misused word; it simply means one who preaches. The more inclusive term is MINISTER or PASTOR *which see*.

PRE-LENTEN SEASON—The period between Epiphany and Lent, which contains three Sundays known simply by Latin numbers; namely, Septuagesima (70), Sexagesima (60), and Quinquagesima (50), each of which is designated according to the approximate number of days by which it precedes Easter. The number indicated, in each case, is derived, not exactly, but according to the

167

decade of days in which the Sunday falls. Quadragesima (40) is the name of the first Sunday which falls within the forty-day Lenten period.

PRIEST—An ordained clergyman who has been employed to administer certain sacraments and authorized to preach and perform other ministerial functions prescribed by the law of the church to which he belongs. This name is used only in liturgical churches. In non-liturgical churches, its equivalent is elder. The Church of England and related bodies have three holy orders: bishop, priest, deacon. The Roman Catholic Church has three "major" holy orders: priest, deacon, sub-deacon. Besides, there are four "minor" orders: acolyte, exorcist, reader, doorkeeper. The Eastern Orthodox churches (Russian, Armenian, Greek, etc.) have five holy orders: bishop, priest, deacon, sub-deacon, reader. The word "priest" is a contracted form of the Greek word *presbyteros,* meaning "elder." The Roman Catholic Church has a hierarchy of clergy with powers superior to priests, but it has no order above that of priest.

PROCESSIONAL CROSS—The cross borne at the head of a procession in a church. In liturgical churches, the person bearing the cross is known as a Crucifer (cross bearer).

PROTESTANT—A name first used for those who protested against the denunciation of the Reformation by Charles V, in A.D. 1529. The name was thereafter loosely applied to the various sects formed after separation from the Church of Rome.

PULPIT—From the Latin *pulpitum,* meaning "a platform." The desk in a church from which the sermon is delivered.

QUATREFOIL—A carving or ornament in four equal parts, or a window resembling a leaf with four lobes. Frequently used in ecclesiastical buildings.

REREDOS—The ornamental screen or decorated backpiece on the wall behind an altar and rising above it. The word means, literally, "behind at the back." *See* DOSSAL.

RETABLE—A kind of shelf or table, in front of the reredos, resting on the altar, and rising a short distance above it. It is used to support a cross and candlesticks, and is frequently raised somewhat in the center where the cross is placed. The name is also applied to a small stand on which the cross is placed to give it elevation.

ROBE—The black pulpit vestment worn by ministers in many Protestant churches during the services of public worship. The word "robe" is preferred rather than "gown."

RUBRIC—Directions for the conduct of ceremonies found in all liturgical books. These were originally printed in red, in order to distinguish them from the text of the ritual; hence, the name.

SACERDOTAL—In the celebration of Holy Communion or the Eucharist in Catholic Churches, the priest is said to offer the bread, often called "the host" (from the Latin *hostia,* meaning "victim of sacrifice"), and the wine as an "unbloody sacrifice" upon the altar. In consecrating and offering these elements, it is believed that "the Real Presence" of Christ enters both species. The power to bring this miraculous transformation to pass is said to be transmitted to the priest by ordination and is termed "sacerdotal." (The word "sacerdotal" is derived from the Latin *sacer,* meaning "holy," and *do,* meaning "offer.") In Catholic Churches, the Eucharistic rite is in the nature of sacred drama. The Doctrine of "the Real Presence" is the chief feature that distinguishes the Catholic Mass from the Lord's Supper as administered in evangelical churches, although there are other more or less important points of difference. Even the form of administration prescribed by John Calvin followed closely the usage of the early Catholic Church: the confession of sin; words of pardon and absolution; a Psalm, a prayer for grace; the Scripture reading; sermon; collection of gifts for the poor; prayer of intercession; the Lord's Prayer; the Apostles' Creed; consecration of the elements and Communion; post-communion hymn; thanksgiving; Nunc Dimittis; Benediction. The Methodist ritual for Holy Communion, in the main, follows the Protestant Episcopal form which, in turn, is based on pre-reformation usage.[6] Thus it is apparent that the basic difference between the Evangelical and the Catholic administration of Holy Communion is concerned with the assumption of sacerdotal power. "Till the beginning of the third century, Christianity corresponded both in idea and spirit

[6] Nolan B. Harmon, Jr., *The Rites and Ritual of Episcopal Methodism,* Cokesbury Press, 1926.

169

to the Judaism of prophecy, the entire sanctified people constituting a holy priesthood unto God. After the beginning of the third century, the idea and form of sacerdotal Judaism, which afterward characterized the Latin Church, were revived." [7] *See* EVANGELICAL.

SACRISTY—The room where the communion vessels, linens and other equipment is kept in a church. The word is derived from the Latin *sacra,* meaning "sacred." Sometimes the same room serves as both vestry and sacristy.

SANCTUARY—A word derived from the Latin *sanctuarium,* meaning "holy place." The word is very loosely used in most evangelical churches. It is perhaps most frequently and wrongly applied to the whole house of worship. More strictly and properly applied, it refers to the part of the church about the altar or communion table. In some of the recently erected church buildings, which are cross-shaped, the sanctuary and the chancel are combined in the head or "eastern" part of the cross. The practice of separating the chancel and the sanctuary is not in favor in evangelical churches, because many think that it is suggestive of priestly separation from the people. The idea of the sanctuary as a kind of "holy of holies" (*sanctum sanctorum*) is derived from the structure of the Jewish temple at Jerusalem.

SEXTON—A word which is apparently a corruption of sacristan, a person or official of a church that looks after the care of the interior of the church, the churchyard, etc. As the name indicates, he was formerly given charge of the "sacred" Communion vessels and other valuables of the church. This function is now generally committed to others.

SHROVE TUESDAY—The day before Lent, so named from the custom of being confessed and shriven (subjected to penance) immediately before beginning the penitential season.

SURPLICE—The full-sleeved linen vestment, reaching to the knees, worn over a cassock by ministers in certain churches. Also worn by members of the choir in liturgical churches. Surpliced choirs may now be seen in the churches of many non-liturgical denominations.

[7] Chas. W. Bennett, *Christian Archeology,* Eaton and Mains, New York, p. 79.

TE DEUM LAUDAMUS—The first words in Latin of a magnificent hymn of praise to the Holy Trinity, worded somewhat in the form of a creed. Its authorship is credited to St. Ambrose, Bishop of Milan (A.D. 340–397). The usual English translation of it, found in the *Book of Common Prayer,* is frequently sung by choirs in the churches of nearly all denominations. It is particularly appropriate for an Easter service.

TRANSEPT—In a cross-shaped church, the transepts are the portions of the transverse cross-bar which project beyond the "north" and "south" of the nave, respectively (see plate M). The name "transept" is applied to the entire transverse section. In a good many churches of this type, the projection appears very much abbreviated when considered in proportion to the length of the nave.

TRINITY SUNDAY—The Sunday following Pentecost, in the Christian Year. It is observed in honor of the Holy Trinity.

VERSICLES (little verses)—A series of short liturgical sentences to be said or chanted in alternation by the minister and the congregation during public worship. For example:

> MINISTER: *The Lord be with you.*
> PEOPLE: *And with thy spirit.*

VESTMENTS—See chapter entitled "Symbolism of a Church" for a discussion of ecclesiastical vestments. Look up the word "Vestments" in a standard dictionary with illustrations. In most of the evangelical churches, ministerial vestments are simple and are likely to remain so for a long time. In the evangelical mind, elaborate vestments are associated with sacerdotal functions.

VESTRY—A wardrobe or room where ecclesiastical vestments are kept. Also, in Anglican, Protestant Episcopal, and some Lutheran churches, the name of the governing body in the parish.

WAFER—A small, round, flat cake, usually of unleavened bread, for use in Holy Communion. The use of unleavened bread is favored for this purpose because it does not crumble when handled.

WHITSUNDAY—Another name for PENTECOST (*which see*). So named because formerly white robes were worn for baptism on that day.

WINE (sacramental)—In the liturgical churches, wine with al-

171

coholic content is used in the Communion Service, but practically all others favor the use of pure, unfermented grape juice. In the liturgical churches, regarding the administration of the elements, particularly wine, there is considerable difference of practice. The clergy of the various Eastern Orthodox churches give the communicant both bread and wine, but the bread is first intincted with the wine by dipping and then distributed. In the practice of the Western or Roman Church, the bread only is given to the communicant and the wine is taken by the celebrant. In the Church of England and related bodies, the elements are given separately to the communicant. The latter practice is generally favored in the evangelical churches.

WORSHIP—From the Anglo-Saxon *weorth,* meaning "worth," and *scipe,* meaning "ship," the reverent acknowledgment, by proper words and acts, of the *worthship* of God. It is regarded as indispensable to the Christian life, which derives some of its greatest values from fellowship in worship. Without integration in the Christian community through public worship and fellowship, the individual Christian can hardly live a typical Christian life, because the Christian life is primarily a partnership concern and not a private interest.

Index

173

INDEX

175

DATE DUE

NOV 14 '64			
H.Scott			
Paisley			
MAY 0 1 1996			
MAR 1 0 1997			
NOV 2 7 2002			
APR 0 3 2003			
OCT 2 0 2003			
GAYLORD			PRINTED IN U.S.A.